The gourmet's guide to
CHINESE COOKING

by Ann Body

The gourmet's guide to
CHINESE COOKING
by Ann Body

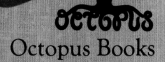

Octopus Books

Contents

First published 1974 by
Octopus Books Limited
59 Grosvenor Street, London W1

ISBN 7064 0153 0

© 1974 Octopus Books Limited

Produced by Mandarin Publishers Limited
14 Westlands Road, Quarry Bay, Hong Kong
Printed in Hong Kong

Introduction

What is it about Chinese food that is so compelling? It reflects the tremendous variety in taste of the Chinese people. Like their art and literature it has a distinct charm of its own. It expresses their delicacy and aim for perfection in the same way as their Ming vases, T'ang poetry and art.

The apparent complexity of Chinese cooking is, to the Westerner, something like an elaborate crossword puzzle: it is as much of a challenge, yet it is very practical, economic and simple to prepare; there are few rules and regulations; no set quantities and measures to abide by; plenty of room for the imagination; above all it is an art to be treated with respect. Every Chinese housewife, from no matter what region or level of wealth, has remembered, perhaps unknowingly, what Confucius said, so never disgraces herself by serving a dish 'overcooked, undercooked, crookedly cut or deficient in seasoning'.

Always discerning and discriminating, the Chinese are able to make something out of nothing. With their inborn sense of harmony they blend a variety of ingredients to produce a dish which excites the palate, rather as an artist blends colours to produce a work of art to be prized by the collector – but the work of a Chinese cook is even more satisfying to more people because, unlike a work of art, it can be eaten.

In preparing this book, I have tried to show that Chinese cooking is not as complicated as it at first seems; that a vast array of unobtainable ingredients is not necessary and that it is fun, as well as a relaxation from the strain of modern living, to enjoy the gentle art of Chinese cooking in which, I am sure, you will find satisfaction.

Firepot

6

Weights and measures

WEIGHTS AND MEASURES

All recipes in this book are based on Imperial weights and measures, with American equivalents in parentheses.

Measures in weight in the Imperial and American systems are the same. Measures in volume are different, and the following tables show the equivalents:

spoon measures: Level spoon measurements are used throughout the book.

imperial	american
1 teaspoon (5 ml.) (tsp.)	$1\frac{1}{4}$ teaspoons
1 tablespoon (20 ml.) (tbsp.)	$1\frac{1}{4}$ tablespoons (abbrev.: T)

liquid measures:

imperial	american	
20 fluid oz.	16 fluid oz.	1 pint
10 fluid oz.	8 fluid oz.	1 cup

METRIC MEASURES

The following table shows both an exact conversion from Imperial to metric measures and the recommended working equivalent.

weight:

imperial oz.	metric grams	working equivalent grams
1	28.35	25
2	56.7	50
4	113.4	100
8	226.8	200
12	340.2	300
1.0 lb.	453	400
1.1 lb.	$\frac{1}{2}$ kilo	
2.2 lb	1 kilo	

liquid measures:

imperial	exact conversion	working equivalent
$\frac{1}{4}$ pint (1 gill)	142 millilitres	150 ml.
$\frac{1}{2}$ pint	284 ml.	300 ml.
1 pint	568 ml.	600 ml.
$1\frac{3}{4}$ pints	994 ml.	1 litre

linear measures:

1 inch	$2\frac{1}{2}$ cm.
2 inch	5 cm.
3 inch	$7\frac{1}{2}$ cm.
6 inch	15 cm.

It is useful to note for easy reference that:

1 kilogramme (1000 grammes) = 2.2 lb. therefore
$\frac{1}{2}$ kilo (500 grammes) roughly = 1 lb.
1 litre roughly = $1\frac{3}{4}$ Imperial pints therefore
$\frac{1}{2}$ litre roughly = Imperial pint

OVEN TEMPERATURES

In this book oven temperatures are given in degrees Fahrenheit with the equivalent Gas mark number. The following chart gives the conversions from degrees Fahrenheit to degrees Centigrade:

°F	°C	
225	110	very cool or very slow
250	130	
275	140	cool or slow
300	150	
325	170	very moderate
350	180	moderate
375	190	moderately hot
400	200	
425	220	hot
450	230	very hot
475	240	

Ingredients

The Chinese divide ingredients into two main types, eating materials, that is meat, eggs, vegetables, seafoods, etc., and cooking ingredients, which are the other substances added during or after preparation to enhance the flavour of the eating materials.

Since most of the eating materials are described in subsequent sections I will deal here with the flavourings or cooking materials used in the following recipes.

It is wrongly supposed that Chinese cooking contains a great variety of exotic spices and herbs. In fact most of the dishes can be prepared with foods readily available in the West, and the relatively few special ingredients which are needed can be obtained easily from a variety of delicatessen shops and some supermarkets in the major towns, or else from any of the Chinese stores springing up in most major cities.

Soya sauce is probably the commonest known Chinese flavouring. It is easily obtainable and with it a tremendous variety of dishes can be cooked. It is always used in Red cooked dishes, which take their name from the reddish-brown colour created by the soya sauce during cooking. There is a substitute for soya sauce, called Vesop and, apart from being readily available, this is considered to be even better than soya sauce for soups and vegetable dishes.

Oyster sauce is fairly widely used, though not nearly as much as soya sauce.

Ve-tsin (monosodium glutamate) is a flavouring or taste powder. A fairly recent addition to Chinese cooking, it is looked down upon by some purists who consider that its use makes all dishes taste the same.

Beancurd and beancurd cheese are used in small quantities, generally in more complex dishes than those given here.

Chinese or dried mushrooms. These are available from Chinese stores and some speciality shops. They must be soaked in hot water or simmered gently before being cut into small pieces and added to the dish.

Ginger is used for flavouring, not usually for eating, and it is the fresh root ginger available in the spring which is used. Rarely is powdered ginger used as a substitute, except in a few of the recipes.

Oil. The most commonly used oils are bean and peanut oil, with sunflower and groundnut oil following closely. The latter is freely available here.

Sesame oil is used much as we use olive oil. It is sprinkled uncooked over food before serving.

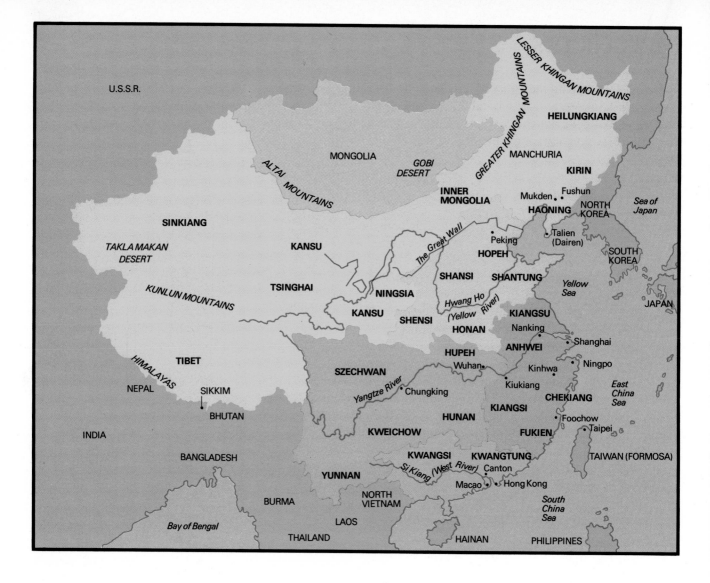

Preparing and cooking Chinese food

Chinese food, like that of every other country, has its regional distinctions.

There are several schools. Cantonese is, perhaps, the best known and certainly includes the greatest variety of dishes. It does not depend on hot spicy ingredients though, of course, it does make full use of soya sauce. It is well known for its steamed delicacies such as dumplings, steamed meat patties, steamed fish, pork and beef; and many dishes from this region are of the quick fried type.

It is the Cantonese who have been largely responsible for the tremendous increase in Chinese restaurants in the West.

Fukien is especially well known for its seafood dishes, also soups and light foods. It is not unusual for a Fukien meal of eight dishes to include at least three soups. This region is also said to produce the best soya sauce.

The Honan region produces richer food than the Fukien region, with a high proportion of hot spicy foods. Sweet and sour dishes are also prevalent, whilst the Szechwan region is different again, making use of fresh hot peppers either during the cooking or in the serving of its dishes.

Whatever the region, the basic preparation and cooking methods remain the same – some of them

Ingredients for Chinese cooking

similar to those employed in the West.

Bearing in mind that the Chinese use chopsticks to eat their food, meat and vegetables are always cut into small pieces – shreds, slices, dice – or, if whole meat such as duck or chicken is being served, it is cooked to such tenderness that it can be easily picked from the carcass with chopsticks. The Chinese consider knives barbarous implements and never, never use them at the table.

Stewing and braising are cooking methods used in China as in the West, but they tend to be longer processes. With the combination of a very low heat and a very long cooking time the Chinese make use of the toughest meat and poultry.

Steaming is a favourite method of cooking many foods, particularly fish, but great care must be taken with the choice of ingredient, since steaming is a test of the quality of the food.

Frying is, perhaps, the commonest form of cooking but it must not be confused with the Western method, which by comparison often renders the food soggy. The Chinese use very little oil or fat and a very fierce heat and it is this speed combined with properly cut ingredients which produces the wonderful crisp texture so much a characteristic of Chinese cuisine.

Red cooked meats

Red cooked meat dishes are rated highly by the Chinese family. They take their name from the fact that soya sauce is always used in the cooking and this gives them their characteristic reddish-brown colour.

The type of meat used is usually pork, though bacon is sometimes used, despite its tendency to be salty. The cut can vary – it can be large joints, such as the shoulder, or the meat can be cut into small pieces, usually cubes and pork chops, though these are not so popular since the tissues are closer and do not absorb the liquid so well. Vegetables are often added during cooking which, compared to stir frying, for example, is a long process.

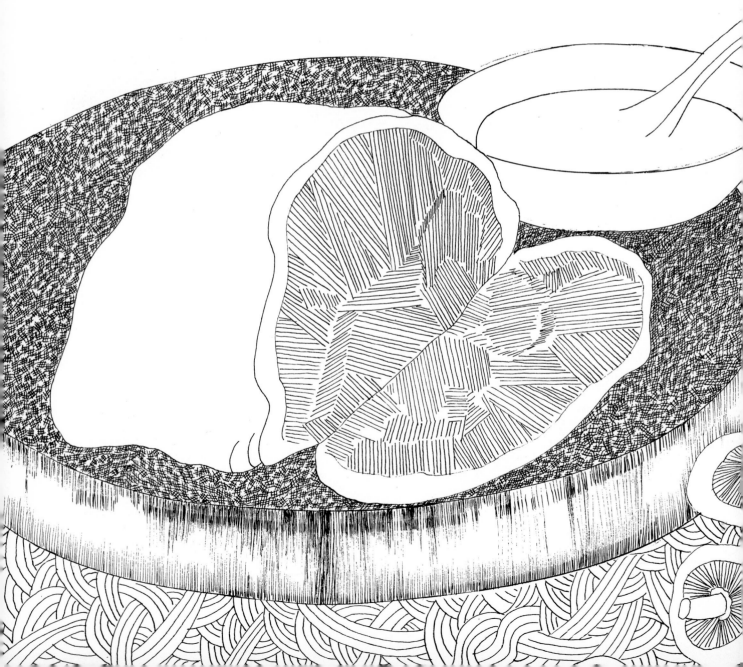

江烷甪

Pork and bamboo shoots

Cut the pork into small cubes. Mix the soya sauce, sherry, sugar and ginger together, add to the pork, toss well and leave for 10 minutes.

Put the pork and flavourings into a large pan, add the water and bring gently to the boil, cover and simmer for 1 hour. Drain the bamboo shoots and shred finely, add to the pan and simmer for another 10 minutes.

Serve very hot.

Note: the liquid can be thickened slightly with 1 tablespoon (1¼T) cornflour (cornstarch) mixed to a smooth paste with a little cold water, if liked.

2 lb. lean pork
3 tablespoons (3¾T) soya sauce
1 tablespoon (1¼T) sherry
1 teaspoon brown sugar
1 teaspoon ground ginger
2 pints (5 cups) water
4 oz. bamboo shoots

Pork and eggs

Cut the meat into 1 inch dice, put into a pan with the water, bring to the boil, remove the scum, cover and simmer for 30 minutes. Add the soya sauce, sherry and salt. Cook for another 30 minutes.

Boil the eggs for 8 minutes, cool and remove the shells. Make a small slit in the side of each egg and add to the pork. Chop the spring onions (scallions), add to the pan and simmer very gently for 5 minutes.

Serve very hot.

2 lb. lean pork
1 pint (2½ cups) water
4 tablespoons (5T) soya sauce
2 tablespoons (2½T) sherry
1 teaspoon salt
6 eggs
6 spring onions (scallions)

Pork and eggs (right)

14

Pork and bamboo shoots (above)

Whole pork shoulder

Wipe the meat and put in a large bowl of cold water to soak overnight. Drain. Put the pork into a large pan with enough water to cover, bring to the boil, remove the scum, cover the pan with a tight fitting lid and simmer for 1½ hours. Add the soya sauce, sherry, sugar, whole spring onions (scallions) and ginger cut into thin slices, bring back to simmering point, cover and cook for another 1 hour.

Serve the pork on a large dish with some of the liquid and pick pieces off with chopsticks or with a fork.

5 lb. shoulder of pork
6 tablespoons (7½T) soya sauce
6 tablespoons (7½T) sherry
1 tablespoon (1¼T) brown sugar
4 spring onions (scallions)
1 oz. green ginger

Red meat plain

Wipe the chops and put them into a large saucepan with the water. Bring to the boil, remove the scum, cover the pan with a tight fitting lid (this is essential to prevent any evaporation of the small amount of liquid) and simmer very gently for about 1 hour. Add the rest of the ingredients and simmer for a further 30 minutes.

Serve immediately.

2 lb. pork chops
½ pint (1¼ cups) water
6 tablespoons (7½T) soya sauce
2 tablespoons (2½T) sherry
1 teaspoon salt
1 teaspoon brown sugar
1 oz. green ginger

Pork and cucumber (right)

Red meat plain (below)

Pork and cucumber

Wipe the meat and cut into small dice. Put into a pan with 1 pint (2½ cups) water. Bring to the boil, remove the scum, cover the pan with a tight fitting lid and simmer for 1 hour. Add the soya sauce, sherry, salt and ginger. Cook for another 30 minutes.

Peel the cucumber and cut into thin slices. Heat the oil and fry the cucumber for 3–4 minutes, stirring all the time. Pile the cucumber in a dish and pour the pork and some of the liquid over.

Serve immediately.

2 lb. lean pork
3 tablespoons (3¾ T) soya sauce
2 tablespoons (2½ T) sherry
1 teaspoon salt
pinch ground ginger
1 large cucumber
2 tablespoons (2½ T) oil

Pork with chestnuts

Cut the meat into small cubes. Put into a large pan with 1 pint (2½ cups) water, bring to the boil, remove the scum, cover with a tight fitting lid and simmer for 1 hour.

Put the chestnuts into another large pan, cover with cold water, bring to the boil, cover and simmer for 1 hour. Drain the nuts, add to the pork with the soya sauce, sherry and brown sugar. Cook for 20 minutes.

Wash and drain the spinach. Put into a frying pan with 2 tablespoons (2½T) of the pork liquid. Cook quickly, stirring all the time for about 5 minutes. Put the spinach into a deep dish and pour the pork and liquid over the spinach.

Serve immediately.

2 lb. lean pork
1 lb. dried skinned chestnuts
4 tablespoons (5T) soya sauce
3 tablespoons (3¾T) sherry
1 teaspoon brown sugar
1 lb. spinach

Pork with chestnuts

1. The chestnuts covered with cold water

2. Bringing the chestnuts and meat to the boil

3. Adding soya sauce to the chestnuts and pork

4. Stir-frying the spinach

Pork and carrots

Wipe and trim the chops. Put them into a large pan with the water, bring to the boil, remove the scum, and cover the pan with a tight fitting lid. Simmer for 1 hour. Add the soya sauce, sherry, salt and ginger. Mix well. Scrub the carrots and cut into 1 inch lengths. Add to the pan and cook for a further 30 minutes.

Serve very hot.

2 lb. pork sparerib chops
1 pint (2½ cups) water
4 tablespoons (5T) soya sauce
2 tablespoons (2½T) sherry
1 teaspoon salt
1 teaspoon ground ginger
1 lb. young carrots

Pork and carrots

1. Trimming the pork

2. Cutting the carrots

20

3. Finished dish

1 and 2. Cutting the meat into small dice

3. Chopping the aubergine (eggplant) flesh

4. Adding the crushed garlic

Pork with aubergine (eggplant)

Wipe the meat, cut into small dice, and put into a pan with 1 pint
(2½ cups) water. Bring to the boil, remove the scum, cover with a
tight fitting lid and simmer for 1 hour. Add 1 tablespoon (1¼T) of
the soya sauce, all the sherry, salt and sugar. Cover and cook for
another 30 minutes.

Cut each aubergine (eggplant) in half lengthwise, remove the
seeds and skin, chop the flesh into small pieces. Heat the oil and
add the aubergine (eggplant), fry quickly, stirring all the time for
3–4 minutes. Add the remaining soya sauce, crushed garlic and
stock. Bring to the boil and simmer for 15 minutes. Pile the aubergine (eggplant) in a dish and pour the pork and some of the liquid
over.

Serve immediately.

2 lb. lean pork
3 tablespoons (3¾T) soya sauce
3 tablespoons (3¾T) sherry
1 teaspoon salt
1 teaspoon brown sugar
3 medium aubergines (eggplants)
3 tablespoons (3¾T) oil
2 cloves garlic
½ pint (1¼ cups) stock

21

Pork with bean curd

Wipe the pork, cut into small dice and put into a pan with 1 pint (2½ cups) water. Bring to the boil, remove the scum, cover the pan and simmer for 1 hour. Add 2 tablespoons (2½T) of the soya sauce, all the sherry, sugar and salt. Cover and cook for another 30 minutes.

Cut the bean curd into 2 inch square pieces. Heat the oil and fry the bean curd for 2–3 minutes, turning it over once during cooking. Add the remaining soya sauce, ½ pint (1¼ cups) water and the onion, cut into small pieces, stir well and cook for 10 minutes, stirring occasionally. Mix the bean curd mixture into the pork and pour into a dish.

Serve immediately.

2 lb. lean pork
4 tablespoons (5T) soya sauce
1 tablespoon (1¼T) sherry
1 teaspoon brown sugar
1 teaspoon salt
½ lb. bean curd
2 tablespoons (2¼T) oil
1 spring onion (scallion)

Pork with mushrooms

Wipe the chops and put them into a large pan with 1 pint (2½ cups) water. Bring to the boil, remove the scum, cover the pan with a tight fitting lid and simmer for 30 minutes.

Soak the mushrooms in hot water for 20 minutes, drain and chop finely. Add to the pan with the soya sauce, sherry, whole onions, sugar and salt. Cover and simmer for a further 45 minutes. Wash the cauliflower and break into florets. Add to the pan, mix well and cook for a further 15 minutes.

Serve immediately.

2 lb. pork chops
4 oz. dried mushrooms
4 tablespoons (5T) soya sauce
3 tablespoons (3¾T) sherry
4 spring onions (scallions)
1 teaspoon brown sugar
1 teaspoon salt
1 cauliflower

Meat slices

Meat slices are tremendously different from the Western idea of sliced meat. The size, and in particular the thickness, is vital to the success of the dish. Each piece must be about one inch square and no more than paper thin, so thin in fact that you can almost see through it. It goes without saying that extreme patience is required – skill is achieved through experience, and if the knife used is a thin bladed one with a razor-sharp edge, then success will be possible without the loss of too many finger tips! Having suffered the frustrations of cutting countless slices not quite thin enough, I would suggest, if I may, that a comfortable stool, a solid chopping block and a constant supply of your favourite beverage will help beginners through this time-consuming preparatory stage. Using the correct cut of meat simplifies the process; tenderloin or pork chops are best.

Pork and mushrooms

Cut the pork into paper thin slices, add the soya sauce and sherry. Toss well. Heat the oil and fry the meat over a fierce heat, stirring all the time, for 2 minutes. Remove from the pan and keep hot. Wash and dry the mushrooms. Slice them thinly and fry quickly in the remaining fat. Add the meat again and mix well.

Mix the cornflour (cornstarch) to a smooth paste with the stock or water, add to the pan and heat gently, stirring all the time until slightly thickened.

1 lb. lean pork
1 tablespoon (1¼T) soya sauce
1 tablespoon (1¼T) sherry
2 tablespoons (2½T) oil
4 oz. fresh mushrooms
1 teaspoon cornflour (cornstarch)
3 tablespoons (3¾T) stock or water

Ham and sweet peppers

Wash the peppers, core them, and cut the flesh into 1 inch pieces. Cover with boiling water for 1 minute; drain. Cut the sliced ham into 1 inch squares. Mix the cornflour (cornstarch), soya sauce, sherry, sugar and stock or water together, add to the ham and mix well so that the meat is completely coated.

Heat the oil and fry the pepper pieces for 2 minutes over a fierce heat, stirring all the time. Remove from the pan. Add the ham to the pan with the liquid, cook for 1 minute, stirring all the time over a medium heat. Add the peppers, cook together with the ham for a further 1 minute.

Serve immediately.

3 sweet peppers
¾ lb. ham
1 tablespoon (1¼T) cornflour (cornstarch)
2 tablespoons (2½T) soya sauce
1 tablespoon (1¼T) sherry
1 teaspoon sugar
2 tablespoons (2½T) stock or water
2 tablespoons (2½T) oil

Pork with mushrooms (right)

Ham and sweet peppers (below)

Cucumber meat slices

Peel the cucumber and cut into very thin slices. Cut the meat into paper thin slices about 2 inches square. Add the soya sauce, sherry, ginger, sugar, salt and pepper to the meat and mix well. Heat the oil and fry the meat for 2 minutes. Add the cucumber and cook over a fierce heat, stirring all the time, for 1 minute.

    Serve immediately.

1 large cucumber
1 lb. pork or beef
2 tablespoons (2½T) soya sauce
1 tablespoon (1¼T) sherry
pinch ground ginger
1 teaspoon brown sugar
pinch salt
pinch black pepper
2 tablespoons (2½T) oil

Pork slices with bamboo shoots

Cut the meat into paper thin slices about 2 inches square. Add the soya sauce, sherry, salt and sugar, toss well.

    Heat the oil and fry the meat over a fierce heat, stirring all the time, for 2 minutes. Mix the cornflour (cornstarch) with the stock or water and add to the pan, off the heat. Mix well. Drain the bamboo shoots and cut into paper thin slices, add to the pan and heat gently for 1 minute.

1 lb. lean pork
2 tablespoons (2½T) soya sauce
1 tablespoon (1¼T) sherry
1 teaspoon salt
1 teaspoon sugar
2 teaspoons (2½T) oil
1 teaspoon cornflour (cornstarch)
2 tablespoons (2½T) stock or water
4 oz. bamboo shoots

Meat Slices with tomatoes

Cut the sliced ham into 1 inch squares. Add the soya sauce, sherry, cornflour (cornstarch) and water, mix well. Heat the oil and fry the meat for 2 minutes. Remove from the pan.

    Cover the tomatoes with boiling water for 1 minute, drain and remove the skins. Cut the tomatoes into thick slices and fry gently in the remaining fat in the pan. Add the ham again and mix well. Heat for 1 minute.

¾ lb. ham
1 tablespoon (1¼T) soya sauce
1 tablespoon (1¼T) sherry
1 teaspoon cornflour (cornstarch)
2 tablespoons (2½T) stock or water
2 tablespoons (2½T) oil
6 large tomatoes

Cucumber meat slices

1. Slicing the cucumber

2. Adding the ginger to the meat

3. Mixing the meat with other ingredients

Cucumber meat slices: Finished dish

Kidney with spring onion (scallion) and cauliflower

Wash and core the kidneys, slice them quickly, and soak in the sherry. Break the cauliflower into very small florets. Cook in salted boiling water for 3 minutes. Drain. Cut the spring onions (scallions) into 1 inch lengths.

Melt the lard and fry the kidneys and onions with the cauliflower for 2 minutes. Mix the cornflour (cornstarch) to a smooth paste with the soya sauce, 2 tablespoons (2½T) water, the sugar, the remaining sherry and the salt. Add to the pan and cook gently for 3 minutes, stirring all the time.

Serve immediately.

4 lamb's kidneys
2 tablespoons (2½T) sherry
1 small cauliflower
4 spring onions (scallions)
2 tablespoons (2½T) oil or melted lard
1 tablespoon (1¼T) cornflour (cornstarch)
1 tablespoon (1¼T) soya sauce
1 teaspoon brown sugar
1 teaspoon salt

Liver and spring onions (scallions)

Wash and dry the liver, then cut into small slices 2 inches by ½ inch. Cover with boiling water for 1 minute. Drain. Mix the cornflour (cornstarch), sherry and soya sauce to a smooth paste, add to the liver and mix well. Chop the spring onions (scallions); wash and slice the leeks into 1 inch pieces.

Heat the oil and fry the liver for 1 minute over a fierce heat, stirring all the time. Add the spring onions (scallions) and leeks, sugar and salt with any remaining cornflour (cornstarch) mixture. Heat quickly, stirring all the time, for 1 minute.

Serve immediately.

1 lb. lamb's liver
1 tablespoon (1¼ T) cornflour (cornstarch)
2 tablespoons (2½ T) sherry
2 tablespoons (2½ T) soya sauce
2 spring onions (scallions)
2 leeks
2 tablespoons (2½ T) oil
1 teaspoon brown sugar
pinch salt

Meat shreds

Making meat shreds is quite a painstaking process. They are
achieved by cutting Chinese meat slices into strips no wider than
the thickness of the slices. They are always quickly cooked
(literally only 2–3 minutes), and are always mixed with other
shredded foods.

Actually, this is an excellent method of making a little go a
long way; again the expensive cuts of meat are used (as for
slices), but when cooked in this way, they offer a greater show
of meat in relation to the other ingredients.

The shreds are generally marinated, then tossed in cornflour
(corn-starch) or egg, or both before being fried over a very fast
heat to separate them; finally the other ingredients are added.

Beef with onions and green peppers

Core the peppers and remove the seeds. Put the flesh into a pan of cold water, bring to the boil and drain. Cut into thin strips; chop the spring onions (scallions) roughly; crush the garlic. Heat the oil and fry the vegetables for 2 minutes, stirring all the time. Remove from the pan.

Shred the beef and fry in the remaining oil for 3 minutes, stirring to brown all over. Add the vegetables to the pan, mix well. Mix the cornflour (cornstarch), soya sauce and stock to a smooth paste, add to the pan and bring to the boil, stirring until thickened.

Serve immediately.

2 green peppers
6 spring onions (scallions)
1 clove garlic
2 tablespoons (2½T) oil
½ lb. beef steak
2 teaspoons cornflour (cornstarch)
2 tablespoons (2½T) soya sauce
2 tablespoons (2½T) stock

Shredded beef heart

Trim the heart, removing all the tubes and blood vessels. Cut the flesh into very fine shreds and soak in cold water for 30 minutes. Drain. Add the soya sauce, sherry, sugar and salt to the heart, mix well. Mix the cornflour (cornstarch) to a smooth paste with the water, add to the heart, mix well.

Heat the oil or lard and fry the heart over a fierce heat for 4–5 minutes, stirring all the time until browned. Chop the onions and ginger, if fresh, add both to the beef and mix well.

Serve immediately.

1 lb. beef or veal heart
2 tablespoons (2½T) soya sauce
2 tablespoons (2½T) sherry
1 teaspoon brown sugar
1 teaspoon salt
1 tablespoon (1¼T) cornflour (cornstarch)
2 tablespoons (2½T) water
3 tablespoons (3¾T) oil or melted lard
2 spring onions (scallions)
small pieces fresh ginger or 1 teaspoon ground ginger

Pork and pepper shreds

Cut the pork into shreds; core and seed the peppers, cut into thin strips; chop the onions. Heat the oil or lard and fry the meat over a fierce heat for 3 minutes, stirring all the time, remove from the pan. Add the vegetables to the pan and cook over a medium heat for 3 minutes, stirring occasionally. Return the meat to the pan with the remaining ingredients. Mix well and cook for 3 minutes, stirring all the time until translucent.

Serve immediately.

¾ lb. lean pork
2 sweet peppers
2 spring onions (scallions)
2 tablespoons (2½T) oil or melted lard
1 teaspoon salt
1 tablespoon (1¼T) soya sauce
1 tablespoon (1¼T) sherry
1 teaspoon brown sugar
1 teaspoon cornflour (cornstarch)

Pork and beanshoots

Cut the pork into fine shreds, sprinkle with half the cornflour (cornstarch), sugar, salt and soya sauce. Mix well.

Chop the spring onions (scallions) finely and fry in the oil or lard for 1 minute. Add the pork and fry over a fierce heat for 3 minutes, stirring all the time. Drain the bean shoots and add to the pan; mix well and heat gently. Mix the remaining cornflour (cornstarch) with the oyster sauce and stock or water, add to the pan and bring to the boil, stirring until thickened.

Serve immediately.

¾ lb. pork tenderloin
2 teaspoons cornflour (cornstarch)
1 teaspoon brown sugar
pinch salt
1 tablespoon (1¼T) soya sauce
2 spring onions (scallions)
1 tablespoon (1¼T) oil or melted lard
large can bean shoots
1 tablespoon (1¼T) oyster sauce
2 tablespoons (2½T) stock or water

Beef with onions and green peppers

Pork and broccoli

Defrost the broccoli and cut it into 1 inch lengths.

Cut the meat into fine shreds; crush the garlic. Add the garlic, salt, sugar, soya sauce and sherry to the meat, mix well and leave for 10 minutes. Heat the oil and fry the meat for 10 minutes over a gentle heat, add the broccoli and cook for 2–3 minutes. Drain the crab and add to the pan, mix well.

Mix the cornflour (cornstarch) to a smooth paste with a little of the stock or water, then add the rest and add all to the pan; bring to the boil, stirring until thickened.

Serve immediately.

$\frac{3}{4}$ lb. frozen broccoli
$\frac{3}{4}$ lb. lean pork
1 clove garlic
1 teaspoon salt
1 teaspoon brown sugar
1 tablespoon ($1\frac{1}{4}$T) soya sauce
1 tablespoon ($1\frac{1}{4}$T) sherry
2 tablespoons ($2\frac{1}{2}$T) oil
7 oz. canned crab meat
$\frac{1}{2}$ pint ($1\frac{1}{4}$ cups) stock or water
1 tablespoon ($1\frac{1}{4}$T) cornflour (cornstarch)

Pork and peanuts

1. Sprinkling the shelled nuts with salt

2. Cutting the pork first into slices

3. Shredding the pork slices into strips

4. Adding the sliced mushrooms and celery and chopped onions to the pan

36

Pork and peanuts

Shell the nuts, sprinkle with salt and fry in the oil for 2–3 minutes. Drain on kitchen paper. Cut the pork into shreds, add the cornflour (cornstarch), soya sauce and sherry. Crush the garlic, add to the meat, and mix well. Heat the oil in another pan and fry the meat quickly, stirring all the time for 2 minutes.

Wash and slice the mushrooms; wash and thinly slice the celery; chop the onions. Add the vegetables to the pan with the oyster sauce, nuts and stock or water. Cook for 3 minutes.

Serve immediately.

$\frac{1}{2}$ lb. ground nuts (uncooked peanuts in husks)
1 teaspoon salt
1 teaspoon oil
1 lb. lean pork
1 teaspoon cornflour (cornstarch)
1 tablespoon ($1\frac{1}{4}$T) soya sauce
1 tablespoon ($1\frac{1}{4}$T) sherry
1 clove garlic
2 tablespoons ($2\frac{1}{2}$T) oil
4 oz. fresh mushrooms
2 sticks celery
2 spring onions (scallions)
1 tablespoon ($1\frac{1}{4}$T) oyster sauce
$\frac{1}{4}$ pint ($\frac{3}{4}$ cup) stock or water

5. Pork and peanuts: Finished dish

魚丸

Meat balls

Meat balls are made from finely chopped or minced (ground) meat – an easy part of the preparation, since a mechanical grinder can be used or the butcher will do it for you. In China they use two enormous chopping knives to achieve the same result – and always with a lean cut of meat, (usually pork) such as tenderloin; the addition of a little fat helps, since meat balls have a tendency to taste dry without it.

They are always small, golf ball size being the largest and walnut size about the smallest, and they are usually served with something else – as the following recipes will show.

Chicken snowballs

Mince (grind) and pound the meat to a smooth paste. Mix half the cornflour (cornstarch) with the water or stock, add salt and pepper, and beat into the chicken until smooth. Separate the eggs and whisk the egg whites until stiff and standing in peaks. Fold into the chicken mixture, using a metal spoon.

Heat the fat and drop teaspoonsful of the chicken mixture into the hot fat. Cook for 1 minute, turning them during cooking to ensure they are evenly browned. Drain.

Put 1 tablespoon ($1\frac{1}{4}$T) of the fat into a shallow pan. Mix the remaining cornflour (cornstarch) to a smooth paste with the stock and sherry, add to the pan and bring gently to the boil, stirring all the time until thickened. Pile the chicken snowballs on a hot dish and pour the sauce over.

Serve immediately.

$\frac{1}{2}$ lb. white chicken meat
1 tablespoon ($1\frac{1}{4}$T) cornflour (cornstarch)
4 tablespoons (5T) water or stock
1 teaspoon salt
pinch black pepper
3 egg whites
deep fat for frying
6 tablespoons ($7\frac{1}{2}$T) chicken stock
1 tablespoon ($1\frac{1}{4}$T) sherry

Plain meat cakes

Mince (grind) the meat finely, add the remaining ingredients and beat well until evenly blended. Shape the mixture into small flat cakes and either fry them in shallow fat or oil for 5 minutes, turning once during cooking, or poach them in shallow stock for 8–10 minutes.

1 lb. lean pork, beef or chicken
1 tablespoon ($1\frac{1}{4}$T) sherry
2 teaspoons brown sugar
1 tablespoon ($1\frac{1}{4}$T) soya sauce
1 egg
1 rounded tablespoon ($1\frac{1}{4}$T) cornflour (cornstarch)
pinch salt
pinch black pepper

Fried meat balls

Mince (grind) the pork very finely; chop the chestnuts, then crush or mince (grind) them finely and mix with the pork. Season with salt and pepper. Add one egg yolk and beat well until evenly blended. Shape the mixture into small walnut sized balls.

Beat the remaining egg and egg white together, dip the balls into it, then in the cornflour (cornstarch); do this twice. Heat the fat and fry the balls for about 10 minutes.

Drain and serve.

$\frac{1}{2}$ lb. lean pork
4 oz. water chestnuts
pinch salt
pinch black pepper
2 eggs
2 tablespoons ($2\frac{1}{2}$T) cornflour (cornstarch)
deep fat for frying

Fried meat balls

1. Shaping the meat mixture into small balls

2. Dipping the meat balls into the egg mixture

3. Dipping the meat balls into the cornflour

Meat balls with cabbage

Mince (grind) the meat and add half the soya sauce, all the sherry, half the salt and the cornflour (cornstarch). Beat well until evenly blended. Shape the mixture into 12 balls.

Shred the cabbage and chop the celery. Heat the oil and fry the cabbage and celery quickly for 2–3 minutes, stirring all the time. Add $\frac{1}{2}$ pint ($1\frac{1}{4}$ cups) water, the remaining soya sauce and salt, and bring to the boil. Place the meat balls on top, cover with a tight fitting lid and cook for 15 minutes.

1 lb. lean pork or beef
2 tablespoons ($2\frac{1}{2}$T) soya sauce
1 tablespoon ($1\frac{1}{4}$T) sherry
2 teaspoons salt
1 tablespoon ($1\frac{1}{4}$T) cornflour (cornstarch)
1 lb. cabbage
1 head celery
oil for frying

Meat balls with cabbage

41

1. Removing the stalks from the mushrooms

2. Preparing the stuffing ingredients

3. Piling the stuffing onto the mushroom caps

4. Placing the stuffed mushroom balls in a steamer

Stuffed mushrooms balls

Cook the mushrooms in boiling water for 20 minutes. Drain, but keep the liquid. Remove the stalks and cut them in thin slices; leave the mushroom caps whole.

Mince (grind) the pork finely, add the soya sauce, salt and half the cornflour (cornstarch) with the sherry. Beat well until evenly blended. Pile the mixture on to the mushroom caps. Place in a steamer and cook for 10 minutes.

Mix the remaining cornflour (cornstarch) to a smooth paste with a little cold water, add the sugar and $\frac{1}{4}$ pint ($\frac{3}{4}$ cup) of the mushroom liquid. Bring to the boil, stirring until slightly thickened.

Arrange the mushrooms on a large hot dish and pour over the sauce.

4 oz. dried mushrooms
$\frac{1}{2}$ lb. lean pork
1 tablespoon ($1\frac{1}{4}$T) soya sauce
1 teaspoon salt
2 tablespoons ($2\frac{1}{2}$T) cornflour (cornstarch)
1 tablespoon ($1\frac{1}{4}$T) sherry
1 teaspoon brown sugar

5. *Stuffed mushroom balls: Finished dish*

Cucumber stuffed balls

Mince (grind) the pork finely, add the egg, salt, half the cornflour (cornstarch) and the sherry, beat well until evenly blended. Peel the cucumber and cut into twelve 2 inch lengths. Scoop out the seeds and pack the pork mixture into the centre of each one. Wash the mushrooms, remove the stalks and place a mushroom upside down over the pork mixture.

Stand the cucumber cups in a shallow pan, add ½ pint (1¼ cups) water, cover the pan and simmer gently for about 30 minutes. Lift the cucumber out on to a hot dish. Keep hot.

Mix the remaining cornflour (cornstarch) to a smooth paste with the soya sauce and a little cold water, add to the remaining liquid in the pan and bring to the boil, stirring until slightly thickened. Pour over the cucumber.

Serve immediately.

½ lb. lean pork
1 egg
1 teaspoon salt
2 tablespoons (2½ T) cornflour (cornstarch)
1 tablespoon (1¼ T) sherry
1 large cucumber
12 fresh mushrooms
2 tablespoons (2½ T) soya sauce

43

Lamb and beef

To the Chinese meat means pork, but they do, of course, eat other meat too. Lamb and beef are used widely, and so too is goat meat, particularly in the south, and probably because of the hilly nature of the area. But generally speaking, if a recipe states 'meat', then you can be sure it is pork meat. Use is made of many different kinds of cuts, which are stated in the ingredients. Lean cuts such as steaks, rump, sirloin and topside, leg of pork, tenderloin and fillet, shoulder and leg of lamb are most popular, and whilst these may be considered the most expensive cuts of meat, remember that Chinese cookery generally calls for only small quantities of any one ingredient, so that the final cost will be no more than if you were using large quantities of a cheap cut.

Steamed beef with rice

Wipe the meat and mince (grind) finely; chop the chestnuts finely; wash and thinly slice the mushrooms; shred the ginger and bamboo shoots; mix all together. Add the sherry, sugar, soya sauce, salt and sesame oil. Beat well until evenly blended.

Cook the rice in salted boiling water for 10 minutes. Drain well. Put into a greased dish and spread the meat mixture on top. Steam in a steamer or saucepan half-filled with salted boiling water for 15 minutes. Break the eggs on top of the beef and steam for a further 10 minutes or until the egg whites are set.

Serve from the dish.

1 lb. rump steak
8 water chestnuts
4 oz. fresh mushrooms
1 oz. green ginger
2 oz. bamboo shoots
1 teaspoon sherry
1 teaspoon brown sugar
1 tablespoon (1¼T) soya sauce
1 teaspoon salt
1 teaspoon sesame oil
1 lb. rice
4 eggs

Barbecue beef

Cut the beef into ¼ inch thick slices; crush the garlic. Mix the garlic, soya sauce, sugar, salt and pepper together with the oil. Add the beef, toss in the mixture and leave for about 20 minutes.

Cook the beef over a charcoal grill or grill under a fierce heat, turning once, for about 3 minutes, depending on personal taste.

1 lb. sirloin steak
2 cloves garlic
2 tablespoons (2½T) soya sauce
2 teaspoons brown sugar
pinch salt
pinch black pepper
1 tablespoon (1¼T) oil

Garlic beef

Cut the beef into strips about 1½ inches long by ¼ inch thick. Crush the garlic and mix with the sugar, soya sauce, stock and sherry. Add the meat, toss well in the mixture and leave for about 30 minutes.

Heat the oil and fry the beef over a fierce heat, stirring all the time, for 3 minutes. Add the remaining marinade and cook for 1 minute.

Serve immediately on steamed rice.

1 lb. fillet steak
4 cloves garlic
1 teaspoon brown sugar
3 tablespoons (3¾T) soya sauce
1 tablespoon (1¼T) stock
2 tablespoons (2½T) sherry
4 tablespoons (5T) oil or melted lard

Beef emit silk

Beat the beef until smooth; chop the onions finely. Mix the beef, onions (scallions), sugar and soya sauce together, then beat well until evenly blended.

Spread thickly over the slices of bread. Bake in a hot oven 450°F, Mark 8 for 10 minutes. Brown under a hot grill for 2–3 minutes and cut each slice in half to serve.

Serve immediately, whilst still piping hot.

1 lb. minced (ground) beef or hamburger beef
3 spring onions (scallions)
1 teaspoon brown sugar
4 tablespoons (5T) soya sauce
4 thick slices French or sandwich bread

Steamed meat pancakes

Wipe the meat and mince finely. Add the remaining ingredients except the eggs and celery, and beat well until evenly blended. Spread the mixture ½ inch thick in a greased shallow dish.

Beat the eggs and pour over the beef mixture. Wash and finely shred the celery, sprinkle over the eggs and cover. Steam in a steamer or saucepan half-filled with boiling water for 25 minutes.

Serve immediately.

1 lb. rump steak
1 teaspoon salt
1 teaspoon sugar
1 tablespoon (1¼T) soya sauce
2 tablespoons (2½T) stock
1 teaspoon oil
1 teaspoon ground ginger
2 oz. bean sprouts
2 eggs
1 stick celery

Preparing steamed beef with rice

Lamb with pea sprouts and spring onions (scallions)

Cut the lamb into strips about 1½ inches long by ¼ inch thick. Toss in the cornflour (cornstarch). Cut the spring onions (scallions) into 1 inch lengths; crush the garlic.

Fry the meat in the oil and salt for 5 minutes, add the spring onions (scallions), crushed garlic, salt and pea sprouts, mix well and cook together for 1 minute. Add the soya sauce, sherry and 2 tablespoons (2½T) water. Bring to the boil and mix well.

Serve immediately.

1 lb. lean lamb
1 tablespoon (1¼T) cornflour (cornstarch)
3 spring onions (scallions)
2 cloves garlic
2 tablespoons (2½T) oil
1 teaspoon salt
4 oz. pea sprouts
1 tablespoon (1¼T) soya sauce
1 tablespoon (1¼T) sherry

Lamb with bean sprouts

Cut the meat into thin slices; crush the garlic and add to the meat with the salt, soya sauce, ginger, sugar and oil. Mix well and cook gently for 3 minutes. Drain the bean sprouts, chop the onions and add to the pan; mix well and cook for 1 minute.

Mix the cornflour (cornstarch) to a smooth paste with ¼ pint (¾ cup) cold water, add to the pan and bring to the boil, stirring until slightly thickened.

Serve immediately.

1 lb. lean lamb
1 clove garlic
1 teaspoon salt
4 tablespoons (5T) soya sauce
pinch ground ginger
1 teaspoon brown sugar
4 tablespoons (5T) oil
4 oz. bean sprouts
4 spring onions (scallions)
1 tablespoon (1¼T) cornflour (cornstarch)

Jellied lamb

Cut the lamb into small pieces and chop the bones up small. Chop the spring onions (scallions) and put into a large saucepan with the lamb, bones and salt. Cover with cold water and bring to the boil, remove the scum, add the soya sauce, cover the pan and simmer for 2½ hours.

Remove all the lamb bones and pick the meat into small pieces, put into a straight sided dish with some of the liquid and press down with a weight on top. Leave until cold and set.

Cut into slices and serve.

3 lb. leg lamb
4 spring onions (scallions)
1 teaspoon salt
4 tablespoons (5T) soya sauce

Lamb with pea sprouts and spring onions

Spiced whole lamb

Wipe the meat and rub salt into the skin. Put into a pan with enough cold water to cover, bring to the boil, remove the scum, cover and simmer for 20 minutes. Drain off the liquid. Mix the soya sauce and sherry together. Crush the garlic; shred the ginger; mix with the soya mixture and rub into the lamb, leave for 10 minutes.

Heat the oil and fry the lamb for about 15 minutes, turning it to brown all over. Add the stock, bring to the boil, cover and simmer for 2½ hours.

Mix the cornflour (cornstarch) to a smooth paste with a little cold water. Lift the lamb on to a hot dish, keep hot. Add the cornflour (cornstarch) to the liquid in the pan and bring to the boil, stirring all the time until slightly thickened.

Pour over the lamb and serve immediately.

3 lb. leg or shoulder of lamb
1 teaspoon salt
1 tablespoon (1¼T) soya sauce
1 tablespoon (1¼T) sherry
2 cloves garlic
1 oz. green ginger or 1 teaspoon ground ginger
4 tablespoons (5T) oil
2 pints (5 cups) stock
1 tablespoon (1¼T) cornflour (cornstarch)

Spiced whole lamb (below)

Beef with celery and cabbage (right)

Beef with celery and cabbage

Wipe the meat and cut into paper thin slices. Mix the cornflour (cornstarch) to a smooth paste with about 2 tablespoons (2½T) water, add to the beef and mix well until the beef is completely coated with the mixture. Heat the oil or dripping and fry the meat over a fierce heat, stirring all the time, for 3 minutes. Remove from the pan.

Wash and shred the celery; wash and finely chop the onions; wash and shred the cabbage. Add the vegetables to the remaining fat in the pan and fry gently for 5 minutes, stirring occasionally. Add the meat, soya sauce, salt and pepper, mix well and cook for 2–3 minutes.

Serve immediately.

1 lb. rump steak
1 teaspoon cornflour (cornstarch)
2 tablespoons (2½T) oil or melted dripping
2 sticks celery
4 spring onions (scallions)
4 oz. white cabbage
1 tablespoon (1¼T) soya sauce
pinch salt
pinch black pepper

Sliced beef with tomatoes

Cut the meat into thin slices, add the egg and cornflour (cornstarch); mix well until coated. Heat the salt, oil and garlic, remove the garlic and fry the beef over a fierce heat, stirring all the time, for 2 minutes. Remove from the pan.

Slice the tomatoes and fry in the remaining fat for 1 minute. Add the beef, tomato ketchup (catsup), sugar, soya sauce and sherry, mix well and bring to the boil. Mix well again.

Serve immediately.

1 lb. rump steak
1 egg
1 teaspoon cornflour (cornstarch)
1 teaspoon salt
2 tablespoons (2½T) oil or melted lard
1 clove garlic
4 large tomatoes
1 tablespoon (1¼T) tomato ketchup
  (catsup)
1 teaspoon sugar
1 tablespoon (1¼T) soya sauce
1 tablespoon (1¼T) sherry

Fried beef in oyster sauce

Cut the meat into paper thin slices; crush the garlic. Mix the corn-flour (cornstarch) to a smooth paste with the soya sauce, add the sherry, salt and pepper. Mix with the beef until all the meat is evenly coated.

Heat the oil with the garlic, then remove garlic from the oil and fry the beef over a fierce heat for 2–3 minutes, stirring all the time. Add the oyster sauce, mix well and add the water. Cook for 1 minute.

Serve immediately.

1 lb. rump steak
2 cloves garlic
2 teaspoons cornflour (cornstarch)
1 tablespoon (1¼T) soya sauce
1 tablespoon (1¼T) sherry
pinch salt
pinch black pepper
1 tablespoon (1¼T) oil
1 tablespoon (1¼T) oyster sauce
6 tablespoons (7½T) water

Stewed lamb with orange

Wipe the meat, then cut into ½ inch dice. Mix the soya sauce, sherry, ginger, orange rind and salt together, add to the lamb and mix well. Put the lamb into a pan with the flavourings and water. Bring to the boil, remove the scum, cover and simmer for 2 hours.

Mix the cornflour (cornstarch) to a smooth paste with a little cold water and add to the pan, bring back to the boil, stirring until slightly thickened.

Serve immediately.

2 lb. lean lamb or mutton
1 tablespoon (1¼T) soya sauce
1 tablespoon (1¼T) sherry
1 teaspoon ground ginger
2 tablespoons (2½T) finely grated orange rind
1 teaspoon salt
2 pints (5 cups) stock or water
1 tablespoon (1¼T) cornflour (cornstarch)

Stewed lamb with orange (left)

Lamb and vermicelli (bean threads) (above)

Lamb and vermicelli (bean threads)

Soak the vermicelli (bean threads) in hot water for 10 minutes. Cut the meat into strips about $1\frac{1}{2}$ inches long by $\frac{1}{4}$ inch wide. Mix the cornflour (cornstarch) to a smooth paste with 1 tablespoon ($1\frac{1}{4}$T) water, add the egg and beat well. Add to the lamb and toss to coat completely.

Heat the oil and fry the meat quickly, stirring all the time, for 2–3 minutes. Drain. Add the vermicelli (bean threads) to the pan, stir well and cook for 2–3 minutes. Mix the soya sauce, tomato ketchup (catsup), sherry, salt and pepper together, add to the vermicelli (bean threads) with the meat. Mix well. Chop the spring onions (scallions) finely, add to the pan, bring to the boil and cook for 1 minute. Add the stock and cook for 5 minutes.

Serve immediately.

4 oz. Chinese vermicelli (bean threads)
$\frac{1}{2}$ lb. lean lamb meat
1 teaspoon cornflour (cornstarch)
1 egg
1 tablespoon ($1\frac{1}{4}$T) oil
2 teaspoons soya sauce
2 tablespoons ($2\frac{1}{2}$T) tomato ketchup
  (catsup)
1 tablespoon ($1\frac{1}{4}$T) sherry
pinch salt
pinch black pepper
3 spring onions (scallions)
$\frac{1}{2}$ pint ($1\frac{1}{4}$ cups) stock

55

Poultry

Chicken is popular in Chinese cookery, closely followed by duck, then goose; though none of them, particularly chicken, is nearly so widely used as in the West.

The Chinese devote almost as much care to devising names for their dishes as they do in the preparation of them. Chicken, in particular, lends itself to one: Chicken of the Three Flavours – so named because of the versatility of one chicken. For chicken is used in three different ways producing three entirely different flavours and often employing different cooking methods for each, such as using the white breast meat in a stir fried dish, some of the dark meat in soup and the rest deep fried.

The Chinese use duck in many more different ways than we in the West. Duck must always be well cooked; for this reason it is rarely stir fried, but slow cooked, as in slow boiling, simmering, roasting or red cooking. Salted duck is also very popular in China, particularly in the Canton region.

Braised chicken with peppers (above)

Chicken livers with prawns and broccoli (right)

Braised chicken with peppers

Core the peppers and cut into thin rings. Fry in the oil and salt for 1 minute. Add 2 tablespoons (2½T) water, bring to the boil, cover and simmer for 2 minutes. Drain.

Cut the chicken into 1 inch pieces. Chop the ginger finely, fry both chicken and ginger in oil for 1 minute. Add the sugar and sherry.

Mix the cornflour (cornstarch) to a smooth paste with the soya sauce and add to the pan. Heat gently, stirring until slightly thickened. Add the peppers and cook for 1 minute.

Serve immediately.

3 sweet peppers
1 tablespoon (1¼T) oil
1 teaspoon salt
1 lb. chicken meat
1 oz. ginger
2 tablespoons (2½T) oil
pinch brown sugar
2 teaspoons sherry
1 teaspoon cornflour (cornstarch)
2 teaspoons soya sauce

Chicken livers with prawns (shrimp) and broccoli

Wash and dry the chicken livers, slice thinly and toss in the cornflour (cornstarch). Heat the oil and fry the livers for 1 minute. Wash and dry the mushrooms, slice thinly, add to the pan and cook for 1 minute. Chop the onion finely and add to the pan with the salt and pepper. Mix well. Cook the broccoli in salted boiling water for 5 minutes. Drain and add to the pan with the prawns (shrimp).

Mix the cornflour (cornstarch) to a smooth paste with the soya sauce and 5 tablespoons (6¼T) water. Add to the pan. Bring to the boil, stirring until slightly thickened. Cook for 3 minutes.

Serve immediately.

8 oz. chicken livers
2 tablespoons (2½T) cornflour (cornstarch)
2 tablespoons (2½T) oil
3 oz. fresh mushrooms
1 spring onion (scallion)
pinch salt
pinch pepper
¾ lb. frozen broccoli
4 oz. peeled prawns (shrimp)
1 teaspoon cornflour (cornstarch)
1 tablespoon (1¼T) soya sauce

Paper (parchment) wrapped chicken

Chop the onions very finely; chop the ginger and mix with the onions, soya sauce, sherry, sugar, salt and pepper. Cut the chicken meat into about 16 slices and toss in the soya mixture. Leave covered for 30 minutes.

Cut out 16 squares of cellophane paper (parchment) (do not use any of the polythene wrappings as these will melt on contact with the hot fat). Wrap each piece of chicken in a piece of cellophane (parchment) and secure. Drop the parcels in hot fat and fry for about 3 minutes. Drain.

Serve immediately.

Note: The correct way to serve the chicken is whilst it is still wrapped. Each parcel is unwrapped only as required by the eater, since the wrapping holds in the flavour and juices until the last minute.

2 spring onions (scallions)
1 oz. green ginger
2 tablespoons (2½T) soya sauce
1 tablespoon (1¼T) sherry
pinch brown sugar
pinch salt
pinch black pepper
1 lb. chicken meat
deep fat for frying

Paper (parchment) wrapped chicken

Boiled chicken

Wash and dry the chicken. Chop the onions roughly; chop the ginger. Put the onions and ginger in a bowl, place the chicken on top and sprinkle with salt. Place the bowl in a steamer or saucepan half-filled with water, cover and bring to the boil. Simmer for 2–3 hours. Add the sherry and cook for another hour.

Add the soya sauce, if liked, just before serving. Serve the chicken in the bowl and pull pieces from it, dipping each piece in the chicken liquor before eating.

4 lb. chicken
8 spring onions (scallions)
1 oz. ginger
1 teaspoon salt
4 tablespoons (5T) sherry
1 tablespoon (1¼T) soya sauce (optional)

Sweet chicken wings with oyster sauce (above)

Duck with almonds (right)

62

Sweet chicken wings with oyster sauce

Wash and dry the chicken wings. Put into a pan with enough cold water to cover, bring to the boil, cover and simmer for 10 minutes. Drain.

Put the chicken wings back into a clean pan, add the oyster sauce, soya sauce, chicken stock, salt and sugar. Bring gently to the boil and simmer for 20 minutes.

Chop the ginger very finely; add the salt and pepper. Sprinkle over the chicken and serve.

1 lb. chicken wings
3 tablespoons (3¾T) oyster sauce
1 tablespoon (1¼T) soya sauce
½ pint (1¼ cups) chicken stock
pinch salt
1 teaspoon brown sugar
1 oz. ginger
pinch black pepper
1 teaspoon coarse salt

Chicken balls with oyster sauce

Cut the chicken into neat pieces as near to ball shapes as possible. Chop the spring onions (scallions) finely, then mix with the soya sauce, sherry and salt. Mix the cornflour (cornstarch) to a smooth paste with the water add the spring onion mixture and mix into the chicken. Mix well. Heat the oil and fry the chicken over a fierce heat for 1 minute, stirring all the time. Add the oyster sauce, mix well, and fry gently for about 5 minutes.

Serve immediately.

1 lb. chicken meat
2 spring onions (scallions)
2 tablespoons (2½T) soya sauce
1 tablespoon (1¼T) sherry
pinch salt
1 tablespoon (1¼T) cornflour (cornstarch)
2 tablespoons (2½T) water
2 tablespoons (2½T) oil
3 tablespoons (3¾T) oyster sauce

Chicken dice with fried walnuts

Soak the mushrooms in hot water for 10 minutes. Chop the walnuts and fry in 2 tablespoons (2½T) of the oil for 2 minutes; drain on thick kitchen paper to remove all traces of oil.

Cut the chicken meat into small pieces, fry in the remaining oil for 3 minutes over a fierce heat, stirring all the time. Mix the cornflour (cornstarch) to a smooth paste with the sherry, soya sauce, salt and sugar. Add to the chicken and mix well.

Drain the mushrooms and chop roughly, add to the pan and cook for 2 minutes. Add the walnuts.

Serve immediately.

4 Chinese mushrooms
4 oz. shelled walnuts
4 tablespoons (5T) oil
3 lb. chicken
1 teaspoon cornflour (cornstarch)
1 tablespoon (1¼T) sherry
2 tablespoons (2½T) soya sauce
1 teaspoon salt
1 teaspoon brown sugar

Ham and mushroom stuffed chicken

Separate the two muscles forming each chicken breast to make eight pieces. Make a split in each one to form a pocket. Mince (grind) the ham and mushrooms together, divide between the pockets and press the edges together. Lay the pieces in a shallow, greased dish. Add the stock and sherry. Steam for 30 minutes. Lift the chicken on to a hot dish and keep hot.

Mix the cornflour (cornstarch) to a smooth paste with the soya sauce. Add the cooking liquor to the soya mixture, bring to the boil, stirring until slightly thickened. Cook for 1 minute and pour over the chicken.

Serve immediately.

4 chicken breasts
2 slices ham
2 oz. mushrooms
¼ pint (⅝ cup) chicken stock
1 tablespoon (1¼T) sherry
1 teaspoon cornflour (cornstarch)
1 tablespoon (1¼T) soya sauce
1 teaspoon sesame oil

Fried chicken slices with mushrooms

Cut the chicken into paper thin slices and put into a bowl. Mix the sherry, salt and soya sauce together and add to the chicken. Chop the ginger and spring onion (scallion) finely and add to the chicken.

Mix the cornflour (cornstarch) to a smooth paste with the water, add to the chicken. Mix well and leave in a cool place for 30 minutes.

Wash and dry the mushrooms, cut into thin slices. Fry the mushrooms in 1 tablespoon (1¼T) oil for 2 minutes, stirring all the time. Remove and keep hot. Add the remaining oil to the pan, heat and add the chicken; fry over a fierce heat for 1 minute, stirring all the time. Add the mushrooms, cook over a gentle heat for 3 minutes.

Serve immediately.

1 lb. chicken meat
1 tablespoon (1¼T) sherry
1 teaspoon salt
1 tablespoon (1¼T) soya sauce
1 oz. ginger
1 spring onion (scallion)
1 tablespoon (1¼T) cornflour (cornstarch)
2 tablespoons (2½T) water
8 oz. fresh mushrooms
4 tablespoons (5T) oil

Fried spring chicken

Cut the chicken into small pieces, removing the bones and skin. Chop the spring onions (scallions) finely and mix with the sherry, soya sauce, salt and sugar. Add the chicken, mix well, cover, and leave in a cold place for about 30 minutes.

Drain the chicken and dip each piece in rice flour. Heat the fat and fry the chicken for 2–3 minutes or until golden, then drain.

Serve immediately.

2 small chickens
3 spring onions (scallions)
2 tablespoons (2½T) sherry
3 tablespoon (3¾T) soya sauce
1 teaspoon salt
1 teaspoon brown sugar
4 tablespoons (5T) rice flour
deep fat for frying

Velvet chicken

Cut the chicken into neat pieces. Mix the cornflour (cornstarch) to a smooth paste with the stock. Beat the egg white and stir into the cornflour (cornstarch) mixture. Add the chicken, mix well and leave for 5 minutes.

Cook the peas in salted boiling water for 5 minutes. Drain. Wash and slice the mushrooms. Poach the chicken in shallow water for about 5 minutes. Drain. Put the chicken, peas and mushrooms into a clean pan with the stock; bring gently to the boil and cook for 10 minutes.

Mix the remaining cornflour (cornstarch) to a smooth paste with the salt, pepper, soya sauce and 3 tablespoons ($3\frac{1}{4}$T) cold water. Add to the pan and bring back to the boil, stirring until thick.

Serve immediately.

1 lb. chicken meat
6 tablespoons ($7\frac{1}{2}$T) cornflour (cornstarch)
$\frac{1}{4}$ pint ($\frac{5}{8}$ cup) stock
1 egg white
$\frac{3}{4}$ lb. frozen peas
4 oz. fresh mushrooms
$\frac{1}{2}$ pint ($1\frac{1}{4}$ cups) chicken stock
pinch salt
pinch pepper
1 tablespoon ($1\frac{1}{4}$T) soya sauce

Chicken livers with almonds

Chop the onion finely and fry in the oil for 1 minute. Slice the chestnuts and add to the pan; slice the bamboo shoots and add to the pan, fry for 1 minute.

Wash the livers and cook in boiling salted water for 3 minutes. Drain, but keep $\frac{1}{2}$ pint of the liquid. Slice the livers and add to the pan. Mix well.

Mix the cornflour (cornstarch) to a smooth paste with the soya sauce, salt and sugar, gradually adding the chicken liver liquid. Add to the pan and bring gently to the boil, stirring until slightly thickened. Add the almonds.

Serve immediately.

3 spring onions (scallions)
2 tablespoons ($2\frac{1}{2}$T) oil
6 water chestnuts
2 oz. bamboo shoots
$\frac{1}{2}$ lb. chicken livers
1 teaspoon cornflour (cornstarch)
1 tablespoon ($1\frac{1}{4}$T) soya sauce
$\frac{1}{2}$ teaspoon salt
1 teaspoon brown sugar
3 oz. blanched split almonds

Chicken livers with almonds

1. Slicing the water chestnuts and bamboo shoots

2. Adding the almonds to the pan

3. Stirring in the almonds

Fried chicken with pineapple

Fried chicken with pineapple

Drain the pineapple and cut the flesh into small pieces. Heat the oil and fry the pineapple for 2–3 minutes. Add the stock and simmer for 5 minutes. Cut the chicken into paper thin slices.

Mix the cornflour (cornstarch) to a smooth paste with the water, sherry, soya sauce and sugar; add to the pineapple with the chicken. Stir until slightly thickened. Cook for 3 minutes.

Sprinkle with sesame oil and serve immediately.

15 oz. can pineapple pieces
1 tablespoon (1¼T) oil
6 tablespoons (7½T) chicken stock
½ lb. chicken meat
1 teaspoon cornflour (cornstarch)
2 tablespoons (2½T) water
1 tablespoon (1¼T) sherry
1 tablespoon (1¼T) soya sauce
1 teaspoon brown sugar
1 teaspoon sesame oil

1. Ingredients for this dish

2. Cutting the chicken into pieces

Red cooked chicken with chestnuts

Cook the chestnuts in 2 pints (5 cups) boiling water for about 2 hours. Remove the brown skins and leave the nuts in the water.

Meanwhile cut the chicken into neat small pieces. Fry them in hot oil for about 5 minutes, or until lightly browned all over. Add the remaining ingredients with the exception of the brown sugar and cover the pan tightly. Simmer for 30 minutes. Add the chestnuts and half the liquid with the brown sugar. Bring to the boil, cover and simmer for 10 minutes.

Serve very hot.

1 lb. dried chestnuts
5 lb. chicken
3 tablespoons ($3\frac{3}{4}$T) oil
1 pint ($2\frac{1}{2}$ cups) water
4 tablespoons (5T) soya sauce
2 tablespoons ($2\frac{1}{2}$T) sherry
1 oz. ginger
1 spring onion (scallion)
1 teaspoon brown sugar

Sweet and sour chicken

Cut the chicken into tiny pieces or mince (grind) coarsely. Mix the soya sauce, sugar, and sherry together. Chop the onion and add to the soya mixture with the chicken. Toss well. Beat the egg and dip the chicken in it. Toss in the cornflour (cornstarch).

Fry the chicken pieces in fat for 2–3 minutes. Drain. Pile on a hot dish and pour the sauce over.

Serve immediately.

1 lb. chicken meat
1 tablespoon ($1\frac{1}{4}$T) soya sauce
pinch brown sugar
1 tablespoon ($1\frac{1}{4}$T) sherry
1 spring onion (scallion)
1 egg
1 tablespoon ($1\frac{1}{4}$T) cornflour (cornstarch)
deep fat for frying
sweet and sour sauce (see sweet and sour cabbage, page 96)

Duck with prawn (shrimp) sauce

Cut the duck meat into paper thin slices. Mix the sherry, salt and pepper, ginger and crushed garlic together in a shallow dish. Add the duck, toss well in the mixture and leave for 5 minutes. Beat the egg, add to the duck and mix well until the duck is completely coated with egg. Add half the cornflour (cornstarch) and mix well. Heat the fat and fry the duck pieces for about 3 minutes. Drain and keep hot.

Chop the prawns (shrimp) finely, add the soya sauce and put into a clean pan with the stock, heat gently.

Mix the remaining cornflour (cornstarch) to a smooth paste with a little cold water, add to the pan and bring to the boil, stirring all the time until thickened. Pile the duck on a large dish and pour the sauce over. Finely chop the spring onions (scallions) and sprinkle over the duck.

Serve immediately.

½ lb. duck meat
1 tablespoon (1¼T) sherry
pinch salt
pinch black pepper
½ teaspoon ground ginger
1 clove garlic
1 egg
2 tablespoons (2½T) cornflour (cornstarch)
deep fat for frying
4 oz. prawns (shrimp)
1 teaspoon soya sauce
½ pint (1¼ cups) chicken stock
2 spring onions (scallions)

Sweet and sour duck

Wash and dry the duck, season well with salt. Beat the eggs, dip the joints in the egg, then in the cornflour. Do this twice. Heat the fat and fry the duck for about 10 minutes or until tender. Drain and keep hot.

Chop the spring onion (scallion) finely; drain the pineapple, but keep the juice; shred the pineapple finely. Heat the oil and fry the spring onion (scallion) and pineapple for 1 minute, stirring all the time. Add the soya sauce, vinegar, sugar, salt and pepper, mix well.

Mix the cornflour (cornstarch) to a smooth paste with a little of the pineapple juice, add more to make up to ¼ pint (⅝ cup) and add to the pan, bring to the boil, stirring until thickened.

Pile the duck on a hot plate and pour the sauce over.

1 duck, jointed
1 teaspoon salt
2 eggs
3 tablespoons (3¾T) cornflour (cornstarch)
deep fat for frying
1 spring onion (scallion)
7 oz. can pineapple
1 tablespoon (1¼T) oil
1 tablespoon (1¼T) soya sauce
1 tablespoon (1¼T) vinegar
1 teaspoon brown sugar
pinch salt
pinch black pepper
2 teaspoons cornflour (cornstarch)

Duck with black beans

Mix the cornflour (cornstarch) to a smooth paste with the soya sauce, sesame oil, salt and pepper. Cut the duck meat into small dice, add to the soya mixture, mix well and leave, covered, for 10 minutes.

Chop the ginger very finely; mash the beans with a fork; crush the garlic; chop the onion finely; mix well together and pound into a paste.

Heat the lard and fry the duck for 3 minutes. Add the paste and fry for 1 minute. Add the stock and sherry, mix well and simmer for 2 minutes.

Serve immediately.

2 teaspoons cornflour (cornstarch)
2 teaspoons soya sauce
1 teaspoon sesame oil
pinch salt
pinch black pepper
6 oz. cooked duck meat
1 oz. fresh ginger
3 oz. black beans
1 clove garlic
1 spring onion (scallion)
2 tablespoons (2½T) oil or melted lard
¼ pint (⅝ cup) chicken stock
1 tablespoon (1¼T) sherry

West lake steamed duck

Shred the cabbage, wash and drain. Chop the ham; add one third of the cabbage with the salt and lotus seeds.

Wash and dry the duck, then stuff with the cabbage mixture, secure the opening and fry gently in the oil for about 20 minutes, turning often to brown all over.

Put the rest of the cabbage in a bowl, place the duck on top and cover with foil. Stand the bowl in a large saucepan, half fill with water and simmer for about 3 hours or until the duck is tender.

Serve the duck on the cabbage immediately.

1 lb. white cabbage
6 oz. ham
1 teaspoon salt
1 tablespoon (1¼T) lotus seeds
5 lb. duck
4 tablespoons (5T) oil

West Lake steamed duck

1. Shredding the cabbage

2. Mixing the shredded cabbage and chopped ham for the stuffing

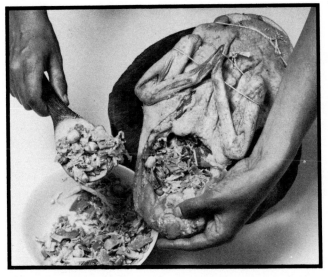

3. Stuffing the duck

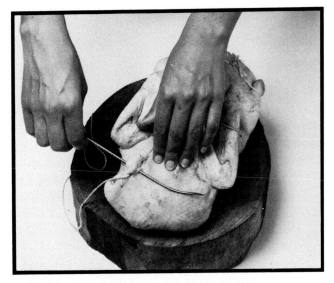

4. Securing the opening

1. Cutting the duck

2. Brushing marinade over the duck
pieces

3. Adding the prepared bamboo
shoots, prawns (shrimp) and
mushrooms to the pan

Braised duck with prawns (shrimp) and bamboo

Wash and dry the ducks, cut small ones in half or large one into
four. Mix the soya sauce, sherry, salt, sugar and ginger together,
brush over the duck pieces and leave for 10 minutes. Heat the oil
and fry the duck for 10 minutes, turning once during cooking.
Drain. Crush the garlic; chop the spring onions (scallions), add to
the pan with the stock or water and bring to the boil. Return the
duck to the pan, cover and simmer for $1\frac{1}{2}$ hours.

Slice the bamboo shoots finely; wash and dry the prawns
(shrimp); wash and thinly slice the mushrooms. Add these to the
pan, bring back to the boil and simmer for 5 minutes.

Mix the cornflour (cornstarch) to a smooth paste with a little
cold water. Lift the duck on to a hot serving dish. Add the cornflour (cornstarch) to the liquid, bring to the boil, stirring until
slightly thickened.

Pour over the duck and serve.

2 small ducks or 1 large one
1 tablespoon ($1\frac{1}{4}$T) soya sauce
1 tablespoon ($1\frac{1}{4}$T) sherry
1 teaspoon salt
1 teaspoon brown sugar
1 teaspoon ground ginger
2 tablespoons ($2\frac{1}{2}$T) oil
1 clove garlic
2 spring onions (scallions)
$1\frac{1}{2}$ pints ($3\frac{3}{4}$ cups) stock or water
2 oz. bamboo shoots
$\frac{1}{2}$ lb. peeled prawns (shrimp)
4 oz. fresh mushrooms
2 teaspoons cornflour (cornstarch)

Onion duck

Wash and dry the duck. Peel and thickly slice the onions, mix
with 2 tablespoons ($2\frac{1}{2}$T) of the soya sauce and push inside the
duck.

Heat the oil and fry the duck gently for 10 minutes to brown
slightly all over. Drain and place in a large pot. Add 2 pints (5 cups)
water, the remaining soya sauce, sugar and the sherry. Bring to the
boil, cover and simmer for 1 hour, turn the duck over and simmer
for another 30 minutes.

Serve immediately.

Note: the liquid in the pot can be thickened with 2 teaspoons
cornflour (cornstarch) mixed to a smooth paste with a little water,
and poured over the duck to serve.

4 lb. duck
1 lb. onions
6 tablespoons ($7\frac{1}{2}$T) soya sauce
2 tablespoons ($2\frac{1}{2}$T) oil
1 tablespoon ($1\frac{1}{4}$T) brown sugar
2 tablespoons ($2\frac{1}{2}$T) sherry

Duck with almonds

Cut the duck meat into paper thin slices. Heat the oil, add the salt and duck and fry for about 5 minutes or until the meat is tender. Add the soya sauce and mix well.

Wash and chop the celery; wash and thinly slice the mushrooms; add both to the pan with the peas, mix well and cook for 1 minute. Add the stock, bring to the boil and simmer for 5 minutes.

Mix the cornflour (cornstarch) to a smooth paste with a little cold water, stir into the pan, bring to the boil, stirring all the time until slightly thickened.

Add the almonds and serve immediately.

1 lb. duck meat
2 tablespoons ($2\frac{1}{2}$T) oil
1 teaspoon salt
2 tablespoons ($2\frac{1}{2}$T) soya sauce
2 sticks celery
2 oz. fresh mushrooms
4 oz. frozen peas
$\frac{1}{2}$ pint ($1\frac{1}{4}$ cups) stock
2 teaspoons cornflour (cornstarch)
3 oz. split, roasted almonds

Fresh ginger duck fry

Cut the duck meat into shreds, that is strips about 1 inch long by $\frac{1}{8}$ inch wide. Put into a bowl with the soya sauce, sherry, salt, cornflour (cornstarch) and water or stock and mix well.

Chop the spring onions (scallions) very finely, shred the ginger, add both to the duck, mix well and leave for 10 minutes.

Heat the oil and fry the mixture quickly over a fierce heat, stirring all the time, for 3 minutes.

Serve immediately.

Note: do not allow this dish to stand at all before serving, since the duck takes on a very unpleasant fishy flavour if left after cooking.

$1\frac{1}{2}$ lb. duck meat
2 tablespoons ($2\frac{1}{2}$T) soya sauce
2 tablespoons ($2\frac{1}{2}$T) sherry
1 teaspoon salt
1 tablespoon ($1\frac{1}{4}$T) cornflour (cornstarch)
2 tablespoons ($2\frac{1}{2}$T) water or stock
2 spring onions (scallions)
2 oz. fresh ginger
2 tablespoons ($2\frac{1}{2}$T) oil

Braised duck with lettuce

Wash and dry the duck. Mix the soya sauce, sherry, salt, oil and ginger together. Pour over the duck and rub well into the skin. Place the duck in a large pan, add 2 pints (5 cups) water, bring to the boil, cover and simmer for $1\frac{1}{2}$ hours.

Shred the lettuce finely and arrange on a large serving dish. Place the duck on top and keep hot.

Mix the cornflour (cornstarch) to a smooth paste with a little cold water. Add the cornflour (cornstarch) to the liquid in the pan and bring to the boil, stirring until slightly thickened.

Pour over the duck and serve immediately.

4 lb. duck
2 tablespoons ($2\frac{1}{2}$T) soya sauce
1 tablespoon ($1\frac{1}{4}$T) sherry
1 teaspoon salt
2 tablespoons ($2\frac{1}{2}$T) oil
1 teaspoon ground ginger
2 large lettuces
2 teaspoons cornflour (cornstarch)

Seafood

Despite the enormity of the Chinese continent, even the most remote inland villages have fresh fish available, fresher than most of us in the West can ever hope to buy. The Chinese buy their fish live and keep them swimming around in tanks until they actually want to use them. And so, with over three thousand miles of coastline providing a tremendous variety and quantity of fish, as well as innumerable village pools and lakes, they make full use of a naturally plentiful food, one which is considered a greater delicacy than meat and poultry.

Fresh fish is generally prepared with wine or ginger to disguise disagreeable fishy flavours. The famous Chinese salted fish is undoubtedly a dish to be tried and enjoyed, preferably in a Chinese home or restaurant, since the unaccustomed smell which accompanies the cooking of salted fish is intolerable to the unitiated Western nose. In fact, Mr. Kenneth Lo, the famous Chinese cookery writer, likens the Chinese attraction to salted fish to the Westerner's inclination to ripe cheeses. Both, he says, belong to the same category.

The Chinese also use much dried seafood; canned abalone, mussels, scallops, shrimps and squids being the most widely used. The recipes in this chapter use mainly fresh fish, or canned fish as an alternative.

'Dragon shrimps' is, characteristically, the somewhat romantic Chinese name for lobsters, and they are a speciality of the Fukien and Chekiang coastal regions. Shrimps abound in many forms in China, most of which are not available here, so shrimps and prawns as we know them are the mainstay of the recipes in that section.

There is a difference between salt water and fresh water crabs, the latter being the type used mainly in Chinese recipes, but since it is often difficult to buy even good quality sea water crabs these recipes generally use canned crab meat as the alternative.

Sole with mushrooms and bamboo

Mix the cornflour (cornstarch) to a smooth paste with a little of the soya sauce; add the rest with the sherry. Beat the egg white until smooth, then stir into the soya mixture in a bowl.

Skin the fish and cut the flesh into strips about 1½ inches long. Toss in the soya mixture and leave for 10 minutes. Fry the fish strips in deep fat for 2–3 minutes. Drain and keep hot.

Chop the spring onions (scallions) very finely; wash and thinly slice the mushrooms; shred the bamboo shoots; shred the ginger (or use ground ginger). Heat the oil or lard and fry the onions, bamboo shoots and mushrooms for 1 minute over a fierce heat. Stir well.

Mix the water with the remaining soya mixture, stir into the pan with the Ve-tsin, heat gently, stirring until slightly thickened.

Pile the fish on a large serving dish and pour the vegetables over. Serve immediately.

1 tablespoon (1¼T) cornflour (cornstarch)
2 tablespoons (2½T) soya sauce
2 tablespoons (2½T) sherry
1 egg white
½ lb. sole fillets
deep fat for frying
2 spring onions (scallions)
2 oz. fresh mushrooms
2 oz. bamboo shoots
1 small knob fresh ginger
2 tablespoons (2½T) oil or lard
2 tablespoons (2½T) water
½ teaspoon Ve-tsin (monosodium glutamate)

Hong Kong plaice (flounder)

Wash and finely chop the spring onions (scallions); shred the celery; thinly slice the chestnuts and cucumber; chop the mushrooms and shred the bamboo shoots. Heat the oil in a shallow pan, add the vegetables and fry over a fierce heat for 2–3 minutes, stirring all the time. Add the stock or water, bring to the boil and simmer for 1 minute. Remove to a hot plate.

Cut the fish into strips about 2 inches long. Put into a greased pan with the sherry and pepper and add the vegetables. Mix the cornflour (cornstarch) to a smooth paste with the water and soya sauce, add to the pan and stir over a low heat until slightly thickened.

Serve immediately.

3 spring onions (scallions)
1 stick celery
2 oz. water chestnuts
2 inch piece cucumber
2 oz. fresh mushrooms
2 oz. bamboo shoots
1 tablespoon (1¼T) oil
¼ pint (⅝ cup) fish stock or water
½ lb. plaice (flounder) fillets
1 tablespoon (1¼T) sherry
pinch black pepper
1 teaspoon cornflour (cornstarch)
1 tablespoon (1¼T) water
1 tablespoon (1¼T) soya sauce

Sweet and sour fish slices

Peel and slice the tomatoes, mix with the pickle. Melt the lard and fry the tomatoes with the pickle for 5 minutes. Mix the cornflour (cornstarch) to a smooth paste with the vinegar. Add the sugar, soya sauce and stock. Add to the tomato mixture, bring gently to the boil, stirring until slightly thickened.

Cut the fish into 2 inch strips. Beat the egg and coat the fish with it, then dip in the flour; do this twice. Fry the fish in deep fat for about 5 minutes, drain and pile on a serving dish.

Pour the sauce over and serve immediately.

3 tomatoes
1 tablespoon (1¼T) sweet pickle
1 oz. (2T) lard (cooking oil)
1 tablespoon (1¼T) cornflour (cornstarch)
2 tablespoons (2½T) vinegar
2 tablespoons (2½T) sugar
2 tablespoons (2½T) soya sauce
¼ pint (⅝ cup) bone stock
1 lb. white fish fillets (whiting, sole, halibut)
1 egg
2 tablespoons (2½T) plain (all-purpose) flour
deep fat for frying

Fish rolls

Skin the fish and cut into fingers about 2½ inches by 1 inch. Make a slit through the centre almost to the other side to form a pocket. Drain the asparagus, keeping the liquor. Chop half the tips and mix with the ham. Press this mixture into each 'pocket', secure with cocktail sticks or thread.

Beat the egg and dip the fish in it, then in half the cornflour. Do this twice. Fry the fingers in hot deep fat for 4–5 minutes. Drain, remove sticks or thread, and keep hot.

Chop the spring onions (scallions) very finely; wash and slice the mushrooms thinly; fry both in a little lard or oil for 1 minute.

Mix the rest of the cornflour (cornstarch) to a smooth paste with a little cold water, stir in the soya sauce and 3–4 tablespoons of the asparagus liquor, mix well and add to the vegetables in the pan. Mix well. Add the remaining asparagus and heat gently, stirring until slightly thickened.

Arrange the vegetables on a large serving dish and place the fish fingers on top. Serve immediately.

1 lb. thick fillet white fish (whiting, sole, halibut)
10 oz. can asparagus tips
2 oz. minced (ground) ham or cooked pork
1 egg
2 tablespoons (2½T) cornflour (cornstarch)
deep fat for frying
1 spring onion (scallion)
4 oz. mushrooms
1 tablespoon (1¼T) soya sauce

Pineapple flounder (plaice)

Cut the fish into large portions. Chop the onions finely and mix with the soya sauce, sherry, salt and pepper. Add the fish and turn in the mixture; leave for 10 minutes.

Mix the cornflour (cornstarch) and egg together to make a smooth paste. Lift the fish from the soya mixture and dip in the egg mixture. Fry in hot lard or oil for 2–3 minutes on each side. Drain and keep hot.

Add the remaining egg mixture to the soya mixture, beating well until smooth. Drain the pineapple and add to the soya mixture with the water. Add to the pan and bring to the boil, stirring until slightly thickened.

Pile the fish on a large plate and pour the sauce over. Serve immediately.

1 lb. flounder fillets (or plaice)
1 spring onion (scallion)
2 tablespoons (2½T) soya sauce
1 tablespoon (1¼T) sherry
pinch salt
pinch black pepper
2 tablespoons (2½T) cornflour (cornstarch)
2 eggs
¾ pint (1⅞ cups) water
10 oz. can pineapple pieces

Splashed fish

Clean the fish and remove the heads. Fry in hot oil for 2–3 minutes. Drain and keep hot.

Add the soya sauce, sherry, salt, and stock or water to the remaining oil, and heat until boiling. Chop the spring onions (scallions) finely; shred the ginger; add to the pan and cook for 1 minute, then pour over the fish.

Serve immediately.

1 lb. sprats
2 tablespoons (2½T) oil
2 tablespoons (2½T) soya sauce
2 tablespoons (2½T) sherry
1 teaspoon salt
4 tablespoons (5T) water or stock
2 spring onions (scallions)
1 small knob fresh ginger

Whiting with soya sauce

Clean the fish and remove the heads. Heat the oil and fry the fish on both sides for about 3 minutes, turning once during cooking. Add salt, pepper, stock or water and soya sauce, stir well and cook for 1 minute. Finely chop the spring onions (scallions), add to the pan and sprinkle with a pinch of Ve-tsin.

Serve immediately.

3 whiting
2 tablespoons (2½T) oil or melted lard
1 teaspoon salt
pinch black pepper
2 tablespoons (2½T) stock or water
3 tablespoons (3¾T) soya sauce
2 spring onions (scallions)
½ teaspoon Ve-tsin (monosodium glutamate)

Fish balls

Skin and bone the fish; chop the flesh finely. Beat the egg and add to the fish with the cornflour (cornstarch); beat well until smooth and evenly blended.

Put the fish stock, lemon juice and oil in a shallow pan, bring to the boil. Chop the spring onions (scallions) and crush the garlic, add to the stock, bring back to the boil.

Shape the fish mixture into small balls, each the size of a pigeon's egg. Lower the fish balls, a few at a time, into the stock, and cook gently for about 5 minutes. Lift out and drain.

Serve immediately.

1 lb. white fish (whiting, sole, halibut)
1 egg
3 oz. (⅔ cup) cornflour (cornstarch)
¼ pint (⅝ cup) fish stock
1 tablespoon (1¼T) lemon juice
1 tablespoon (1¼T) oil
2 spring onions (scallions)
1 clove garlic

Fish balls

1. Skinning the fish

2. Chopping the fish flesh finely

3. Beating the fish mixture

4. Shaping the fish mixture into small balls

5. Lowering the fish balls into the hot stock mixture

Braised eel

Skin the eel and cut into 2 inch lengths. Wash well and fry in the oil or lard for 5 minutes. Chop the spring onions (scallions) finely, add to the eel and fry gently for another 5 minutes. Crush the garlic, add to the pan with the sherry, soya sauce, sugar and salt, mix well, then add the water. Bring gently to the boil, cover and simmer for 15 minutes.

Mix the cornflour (cornstarch) to a smooth paste with a little cold water, add to the pan, stirring until slightly thickened.

Serve immediately.

1 lb. eel
4 tablespoons (5T) oil or melted lard
2 spring onions (scallions)
2 cloves garlic
2 tablespoons (2½T) sherry
2 tablespoons (2½T) soya sauce
1 teaspoon sugar
½ teaspoon salt
½ pint (1¼ cups) water
1 teaspoon cornflour (cornstarch)

Bass with ginger

Wash and clean the fish, removing the scales and fins. Put into a deep pan with the salt, cover with cold water and bring gently to the boil; cover and simmer for 5 minutes.

Wash and finely chop the ginger, or use ground ginger if fresh is not available. Chop the spring onions (scallions) very finely, mix with the ginger, soya sauce and oil.

Lift the fish from the pan, drain and place on a large serving dish. Pour the ginger mixture over and serve immediately.

2 lb. bass
2 teaspoons salt
1 small knob fresh ginger
2 spring onions (scallions)
1 tablespoon (1¼T) soya sauce
1 teaspoon oil

Raw fish strips

Skin the fish and cut into narrow strips about 2 inches long.

Chop the onion very finely and put into a shallow dish with the remaining ingredients, except the pineapple. Add the fish and toss well in the mixture. Leave for 10 minutes.

Lift the fish out of the mixture. Shred the pineapple very finely and mix with the fish.

Serve piled on a large plate.

1 lb. plaice (flounder) fillets (or salmon when cheap)
1 spring onion (scallion)
1 tablespoon (1¼T) sesame oil
2 tablespoons (2½T) sherry
2 tablespoons (2½T) soya sauce
pinch salt
pinch black pepper
1 slice pineapple

Scallops with peppers

Wash the scallops and trim. Cut each into slices. Chop the spring onions (scallions) finely. Heat the oil or lard and fry the scallops and onions for about 3 minutes, stirring all the time. Add the salt, mix well.

Wash the peppers and cut into 1 inch pieces. Add to the pan with 4 tablespoons (5T) water and bring to the boil, stirring. Simmer for about 2 minutes.

Serve immediately.

1 lb. scallops
2 spring onions (scallions)
1 tablespoon (1¼T) oil or melted lard
1 teaspoon salt
2 sweet peppers

Plaice (flounder) with vegetables and almonds

Cut the fish into 2 inch strips, dip in beaten egg, then in flour; do this twice. Heat the oil or lard and fry the fish for 5 minutes. Drain and keep hot.

Wash and slice the mushrooms; chop the onions finely; wash and drain the bean sprouts. Add all the vegetables to the remaining oil or lard and fry over a fierce heat for 2–3 minutes, stirring all the time.

Mix the cornflour (cornstarch) to a smooth paste with the water or stock, add the sugar and soya sauce. Stir into the vegetables and heat gently until slightly thickened.

Pile the vegetables and their sauce on a large dish, arrange the fish on top and sprinkle with the almonds. Serve immediately.

1 lb. plaice (flounder) fillets
1 egg
1 tablespoon (1¼T) flour
6 tablespoons (7½T) oil or melted lard
4 oz. fresh mushrooms
4 spring onions (scallions)
4 oz. bean sprouts
1 teaspoon cornflour (cornstarch)
1 tablespoon (1¼T) water or stock
1 teaspoon sugar
2 tablespoons (2½T) soya sauce
3 oz. sliced almonds, roasted

Scallops with peppers (above left)

Raw fish strips (below left)

Plaice (flounder) with vegetables and almonds (below)

Prawn (shrimp) and pork cakes

Mince (grind) the prawns (shrimp) and pork together. Mix with the remaining ingredients, except the oil, and beat well until smooth. Shape the mixture into small flat cakes. Heat the oil and fry the cakes for 2 minutes on each side. Drain.

Serve very hot with sweet and sour sauce (see sweet and sour cabbage, page 96) if liked.

6 oz. peeled prawns (shrimp)
4 oz. lean pork
1 tablespoon (1¼T) cornflour (cornstarch)
1 tablespoon (1¼T) sherry
1 tablespoon (1¼T) soya sauce
pinch black pepper
½ teaspoon salt
2 tablespoons (2½T) pork stock
2 tablespoons (2½T) oil

Shrimps with green peas

Wash and dry the shrimps, fry in hot oil or lard (fat) for 2 minutes. Thinly slice the ginger; finely chop the onions; crush the garlic. Add to the pan with the shrimps, mix well and cook for 1 minute. Cook the peas in salted boiling water for 5 minutes. Drain and add to the pan. Mix well.

Mix the cornflour to a smooth paste with the soya sauce, salt and water. Add to the pan and bring gently to the boil, stirring until slightly thickened. Add the sesame oil and mix well.

Serve immediately.

1 lb. peeled shrimps
1 tablespoon (1¼T) oil or melted lard
1 oz. green ginger
2 spring onions (scallions)
2 cloves garlic
4 oz. frozen peas
2 teaspoons cornflour (cornstarch)
1 tablespoon (1¼T) soya sauce
pinch salt
2 tablespoons (2½T) water
1 teaspoon sesame oil

Crab Kromeskies with sweet and sour sauce

Chop the crab meat finely; wash and finely chop the onions (scallions); wash and chop the mushrooms. Mix these ingredients with the oyster and soya sauces, sherry and 1 egg. Beat well until smooth. Form into cork shapes.

Beat the remaining egg and dip the corks in it, then in the cornflour (cornstarch). Do this twice. Fry a few at a time in the hot fat for 4–5 minutes.

1 lb. fresh crab meat
2 spring onions (scallions)
2 oz. fresh mushrooms
2 teaspoons oyster sauce
2 teaspoons soya sauce
1 tablespoon (1¼T) sherry
2 eggs
2 tablespoons (2½T) cornflour (cornstarch)
deep fat for frying

Hong Kong crab

Heat the oil or lard, crush the garlic and fry for 1 minute. Mince (grind) the pork finely and add to the pan; fry for 4–5 minutes. Season with salt.

Drain the crab and cut the flesh into 1 inch pieces, add to the pan, mixing well. Cover and cook over a gentle heat for 5 minutes. Add the soya sauce, salt, pepper and stock, and bring gently to the boil.

Mix the cornflour (cornstarch) to a smooth paste with a little cold water and add to the pan, stirring until slightly thickened. Beat the egg and pour in a thin stream into the mixture, stirring all the time until ribbons form. Wash and finely chop the onions and sprinkle over the top.

Serve immediately.

4 tablespoons (5T) oil or melted lard
1 clove garlic
4 oz. lean pork
½ teaspoon salt
two 7 oz. cans crab meat
3 tablespoons (3¾T) soya sauce
pinch salt
pinch black pepper
½ pint (1¼ cups) pork stock
2 teaspoons cornflour (cornstarch)
1 egg
2 spring onions (scallions)

Abalone and celery

Drain the abalone, keeping the juice for soup. Cut the abalone into fine shreds.

    Wash the celery and cut into 1 inch pieces. Put into a pan of cold water, bring to the boil, simmer for 1 minute, then drain. Freshen under cold running water. Drain and mix with the abalone.

    Mix the remaining ingredients together in a bowl. Add the abalone and celery mixture, toss well and serve cold.

2 cans abalone
1 head celery
2 tablespoons (2½T) soya sauce
1 tablespoon (1¼T) brown sugar
1 tablespoon (1¼T) salt
black pepper
1 tablespoon (1¼T) sesame oil (or nut oil)

Lobster with pork

Crush the garlic and heat gently in the oil or lard. Mince (grind) the pork finely and add to the pan, stir well to separate, and cook over a fierce heat for 2–3 minutes, stirring all the time. Mix the soya sauce, salt, pepper and boiling water together, add to the pan and bring back to the boil. Cut the lobster and the shell into neat slices and add to the pan. Cover and simmer for 2–3 minutes.

    Mix the cornflour (cornstarch) to a smooth paste with ¼ pint (⅝ cup) cold water, stir into the pan and bring to the boil, stirring until slightly thickened. Chop the spring onions (scallions) finely. Beat the egg. Remove the pan from the heat, add the onions (scallions) and egg and stir briskly to distribute the egg.

    Serve immediately.

1 clove garlic
3 tablespoons (3¾T) oil or melted lard
½ lb. lean pork
3 tablespoons (3¾T) soya sauce
1 teaspoon salt
pinch black pepper
½ pint (1¼ cups) boiling water
1 lobster tail or 7 oz. lobster meat
2 teaspoons cornflour (cornstarch)
2 spring onions (scallions)
1 egg

Fried lobster with bean sprouts

Wash and drain the cabbage. Shred finely and fry in ~~~~~~~~~~~~~~~~~ white cabbage
for 1 minute over a fierce heat, stirring ~~~~~~~~~~~~~~~~~~~~~~~~~~ oil ~~~~~~
salt and 2 tablespoons (2¼T) ~~~~~~~~~~~~~~~~~~~~~~~~~ 1 teaspoon salt
minutes.

Cut the lobster into 1 inch pieces. Fry in the remaining oil for
2–3 minutes. Add the soya sauce, sugar and sherry, stir well. Mix
the cornflour (cornstarch) to a smooth paste with the water and
add to the pan with the cabbage and its liquid, stirring until
slightly thickened.

Serve immediately.

1 lb. lobster meat
1 tablespoon (1¼T) soya sauce
1 teaspoon brown sugar
1 tablespoon (1¼T) sherry
2 teaspoons cornflour (cornstarch)
6 tablespoons (7½T) water

Braised lobster with cabbage

Cut the lobster into neat slices and season with salt and pepper.
Heat the oil or lard and fry the lobster for 1 minute. Wash and
drain the bean sprouts, then add to the pan, stirring for 1 minute
over a fierce heat.

Mix the cornflour (cornstarch) and sugar together to a smooth
paste with the water and soya sauce. Add to the pan and heat
gently, stirring until slightly thickened. Chop the spring onion
(scallion) finely, add to the pan, mix well.

Serve immediately.

Fried lobster with bean sprouts

½ lb. lobster meat
pinch salt
pinch black pepper
1 tablespoon (1¼T) oil or melted lard
1 lb. bean sprouts
1 teaspoon cornflour (cornstarch)
1 teaspoon brown sugar
3 tablespoons (3¾T) water
1 tablespoon (1¼T) soya sauce
1 spring onion (scallion)

Prawn (shrimp) fritters

Mince (grind) the prawns (shrimp) twice; chop the onions (scallions) finely. Add both to the egg and cornflour (cornstarch), mix to a smooth paste, then gradually beat in the milk. Season with salt.

Heat the fat and drop tablespoons of the mixture into it; fry for 2–3 minutes until golden brown.

Drain and serve immediately.

1 lb. prawns (shrimp)
2 spring onions (scallions)
1 egg
5 tablespoons (6¼T) cornflour (cornstarch)
½ pint (1¼ cups) milk
½ teaspoon salt
deep fat for frying

Prawn (shrimp) fritters

1. Preparing the fritter mixture

2. Dropping tablespoons of fritter mixture into the fat

3. The fritter frying

4. Removing the fritters from the fat and draining

Scallops with pineapple

Wash the scallops and prepare as for Scallops with peppers (see page 81). Mix the soya sauce, sugar and salt together, sprinkle over the scallops and leave, covered, for 20 minutes. Beat the egg until smooth.

Drain the scallops and dip in the egg, then in cornflour (cornstarch). Do this twice. Fry the scallops in deep fat for 2–3 minutes until crispy. Drain and keep hot.

Mix the remaining cornflour (cornstarch) to a smooth paste with a little of the pineapple juice. Add to the remaining soya mixture with the vinegar. Chop the spring onion (scallion) finely and fry quickly in a little lard, then add the soya mixture with 4 tablespoons (5T) water, and the pineapple. Bring to the boil, stirring until slightly thickened.

Pile the scallops on a large plate and pour the sauce over. Serve immediately.

1 lb. scallops
2 tablespoons ($2\frac{1}{2}$T) soya sauce
1 tablespoon ($1\frac{1}{4}$T) brown sugar
1 teaspoon salt
1 egg
2 tablespoons ($2\frac{1}{2}$T) cornflour (cornstarch)
deep fat for frying
2 tablespoons ($2\frac{1}{2}$T) vinegar
1 spring onion (scallion)
10 oz. can pineapple pieces

Prawns (shrimps) with celery

Chop the spring onions (scallions) finely; mix with the prawns (shrimp). Heat the oil and cook the onions (scallions) and prawns over a fierce heat for 2 minutes, stirring all the time. Wash and finely chop the celery; wash and thinly slice the mushrooms. Add both to the pan and cook gently for 2–3 minutes, stirring occasionally. Add the black pepper and soya sauce, mix well.

Mix the cornflour (cornstarch) to a smooth paste with a little of the water, add the rest of the water and stir into the pan. Bring to the boil, stirring until slightly thickened.

Serve immediately.

3 spring onions (scallions)
$\frac{1}{2}$ lb. peeled prawns (shrimp)
1 tablespoon ($1\frac{1}{4}$T) oil
3 sticks celery
2 oz. fresh mushrooms
pinch black pepper
1 tablespoon ($1\frac{1}{4}$T) soya sauce
1 teaspoon cornflour (cornstarch)
7 tablespoons ($8\frac{3}{4}$T) water

Shrimps with chestnuts

Bring the stock to the boil, add the shrimps and simmer gently for 5 minutes.

Chop the water chestnuts roughly, add to the stock with the remaining ingredients. Bring back to the boil, reduce the heat and simmer for 2–3 minutes.

2 pints (5 cups) fish stock
3 oz. dried shrimps
6 water chestnuts
pinch salt
1 teaspoon brown sugar
1 tablespoon ($1\frac{1}{4}$T) soya sauce
1 teaspoon sesame oil

Prawns (shrimps) with peppers

Wash and core the peppers, cut into rings and fry in half the oil with the salt for 1 minute. Add 2 tablespoons ($2\frac{1}{2}$T) water, cover and simmer for 5 minutes. Drain and keep hot.

Heat the remaining oil and fry the prawns (shrimp) for 2–3 minutes. Add the soya sauce, sugar and sherry to the pan. Peel and chop the cucumber roughly, add to the pan and cook for 1 minute.

Mix the cornflour (cornstarch) to a smooth paste with the water, add to the pan, heat gently, stirring all the time until slightly thickened. Add the peppers and mix well.

Serve immediately.

3 sweet peppers
2 tablespoons ($2\frac{1}{2}$T) oil
$\frac{1}{2}$ teaspoon salt
1 lb. peeled prawns (shrimp)
1 tablespoon ($1\frac{1}{4}$T) soya sauce
1 teaspoon brown sugar
1 tablespoon ($1\frac{1}{4}$T) sherry
2 inch piece cucumber
1 teaspoon cornflour (cornstarch)
6 tablespoons ($7\frac{1}{2}$T) water

Prawn (shrimp) cutlets

Hold the prawns (shrimp) firmly by the tail and remove the rest of the shell, leaving the tail piece intact. Split the prawns (shrimp) in half lengthways almost to the tail and remove the intestinal cord. Flatten the prawns (shrimp) to look like cutlets. Sprinkle with sherry.

Beat the egg and dip the cutlets in it, then in the cornflour (cornstarch). Do this twice. Fry the cutlets in deep fat for 2–3 minutes. Drain and serve plain or with a sweet and sour sauce (see sweet and sour cabbage, page 96).

8 Mediterranean (4 Pacific) prawns (shrimp)
1 tablespoon (1¼T) sherry
1 egg
2 tablespoons (2½T) cornflour (cornstarch)
deep fat for frying

Crab with black beans

Drain the crab and chop the meat finely. Arrange it in the base of a greased shallow dish or soufflé dish.

Put the beans in boiling water, bring them back to the boil, then drain and cool under cold running water. Mash them with a fork. Crush the garlic and mix with the beans, sherry, oil and ginger. Beat well to make a smooth paste. Spread this mixture over the crab. Cover the dish. Steam gently for 45 minutes.

Serve from the bowl.

Note: the correct way to eat any solid dish like this is to pinch out pieces from the dish with chopsticks – Westerners usually find a fork easier.

two 7 oz. cans crab meat
1 oz. black beans
1 clove garlic
2 teaspoons sherry
2 teaspoons oil
pinch ground ginger

Prawn (shrimp) cutlets (right)

Crab with black beans (below)

Vegetables

Chinese vegetable cookery is vast, varied and holds a fascination perhaps surpassing any in the world. The Chinese are avid vegetable eaters and take great pains to ensure that their vegetable dishes are crisp, colourful, fresh and full of flavour, all the time.

Many 'meat' and 'fish' dishes are really combinations of meat or fish with varieties of vegetables, particularly the quick cooked dishes – meat slices and shreds etc.

Unlike the Western treatment of vegetables (invariably a cooking session in too much water for too long, after which the liquor containing all the valuable nutrients is thrown away), little or no water is used in Chinese vegetable cookery. Leaf vegetables, such as lettuce and spinach, are cooked in their own juices, without additional liquid; all vegetables are generally cut into very small pieces – either fine shreds or strips – and are cooked very quickly.

Two cooking methods are sometimes employed, as in the case of hard vegetables, which are first fried for a couple of minutes, then have a little water added to produce a combination of frying and braising. Or the methods can be reversed for quick frying over a fierce heat. But in any case, at no time are the vegetables ever overcooked and mushy.

Cold cucumbers, cold sweet and sour radishes, cold asparagus and cold celery (below)

Sweet and sour cabbage (right)

94

Sweet and sour cabbage

Peel and shred or grate the carrot; chop the tomatoes. Heat 1 table-spoon (1¼T) oil in a pan and add the carrots and tomatoes; fry for 2–3 minutes over a medium heat, stirring all the time.

Mix the cornflour (cornstarch) with a little of the stock or water, add the rest and the soya sauce, salt, brown sugar and vinegar. Add to the tomato mixture and bring to the boil, stirring until thickened. Simmer gently whilst preparing the cabbage.

Shred the cabbage and fry in the remaining oil in another large pan, for 3–4 minutes, stirring all the time. Add the sherry, mix well and cook for 2 minutes. Pile the cabbage on to a dish and pour the sauce over.

Serve immediately.

1 large carrot
3 tomatoes
3 tablespoons (3¾T) oil or melted lard
1 tablespoon (1¼T) cornflour (cornstarch)
¼ pint (⅝ cup) stock or water
2 tablespoons (2½T) soya sauce
1 teaspoon salt
1 tablespoon (1¼T) brown sugar
2 tablespoons (2½T) wine vinegar
1 Chinese cabbage or hard white cabbage
2 tablespoons (2½T) sherry

Cold asparagus

Wash the asparagus and cut off the tough part of the stems. Put into a large pan, cover with boiling water and bring back to the boil. Simmer for 5 minutes. Drain. Rinse immediately under cold running water until completely cold. Drain well.

Put the asparagus into a serving dish, add the soya sauce, sugar oil and salt, mix well and serve as a salad.

1 lb. asparagus
2 tablespoons (2½T) soya sauce
1 teaspoon brown sugar
1 tablespoon (1¼T) olive oil
pinch salt

Cold celery

Scrub the celery and cut into 1 inch lengths. Put into a large pan, cover with cold water, bring to the boil, drain and immediately cover with cold water. Chill completely under cold running water. Drain. Add the salt, soya sauce, sugar and sesame oil.

Mix well and serve very cold.

1 head celery
pinch salt
1 tablespoon (1¼T) soya sauce
1 teaspoon brown sugar
1 teaspoon sesame oil

Cold cucumber

Peel the cucumber and cut into small dice. Sprinkle with the remaining ingredients and leave for 5 minutes before serving. Make sure the sugar has dissolved before serving.

1 cucumber
½ teaspoon salt
1 tablespoon (1¼T) soya sauce
1 tablespoon (1¼T) wine vinegar
1 tablespoon (1¼T) caster (superfine) sugar
2 teaspoons sesame oil

Cold sweet and sour radishes

Wash, top and tail the radishes; drain. Using the handle end of a heavy kitchen knife, smash each radish, but do not break them completely – they must remain almost whole. Sprinkle with salt and leave for 5 minutes. Add the remaining ingredients, mix well and, when the sugar has dissolved, mix again.

Serve chilled.

2 bunches small radishes
1 teaspoon salt
2 tablespoons (2½T) soya sauce
1 tablespoon (1¼T) wine vinegar
1 tablespoon (1¼T) brown sugar
2 teaspoons sesame oil

Cauliflower, water chestnuts and mushrooms

Wash the cauliflower and break into florets, cover with boiling water and leave for 5 minutes. Drain. Cut the chestnuts into large pieces.

Cover the mushrooms with ½ pint (1¼ cups) boiling water, cover and leave for 30 minutes. Drain, reserve the water; cut the mushrooms into thin slices. Heat the oil and fry the mushrooms for 2–3 minutes over a fierce heat, stirring all the time. Add the chestnuts and cauliflower, mix well and cook for 2 minutes.

Mix the cornflour (cornstarch) to a smooth paste with the remaining ingredients, add the mushroom water. Add to the pan and bring to the boil, stirring all the time until thickened. Cook for 2–3 minutes.

Serve immediately.

1 small cauliflower
8 water chestnuts
6 dried mushrooms
2 tablespoons (2½T) oil
2 tablespoons (2½T) cornflour (cornstarch)
2 tablespoons (2½T) soya sauce
2 tablespoons (2½T) sherry
2 tablespoons (2½T) stock

Fried lettuce

Wash and trim the lettuce and shake off excess moisture. Cut into four. Heat the oil and fry the lettuce for 1 minute. Add the crushed garlic, salt and Vesop, mix well and cook for another 1 minute.

Serve immediately.

1 large lettuce
1 tablespoon (1¼T) oil
2 cloves garlic
pinch salt
1 teaspoon Vesop

Chinese vegetables

Braised turnips

Thickly peel the turnips and cut them into small dice. Heat the oil or lard and fry the turnips for 3 minutes. Chop the onions (scallions) and add to the pan, mix well. Add the stock, meat extract, soya sauce and sugar, mix well. Cover the pan and simmer for 5 minutes.

Sprinkle with black pepper and serve immediately.

1 lb. young turnips
2 tablespoons (2½T) oil or melted lard
2 spring onions (scallions)
¼ pint (⅝ cup) stock
1 teaspoon meat extract
2 tablespoons (2½T) soya sauce
1 teaspoon brown sugar
pinch black pepper

Fried mushrooms and bamboo shoots

Soak the mushrooms in boiling water for 30 minutes. Drain and slice. Heat the oil and fry the mushrooms for 3 minutes. Remove from the pan.

Drain the bamboo shoots and cut into slices, add to the remaining oil with the salt, sherry and Vesop. Bring gently to the boil and simmer for 3 minutes.

Mix the cornflour (cornstarch) to a smooth paste with a little of the mushroom water, make up to ¼ pint (⅝ cup) and add to the pan with the mushrooms; cover and simmer for 10 minutes. Arrange on a large dish and sprinkle with ham.

Serve immediately.

12 dried mushrooms
2 tablespoons (2½T) oil
8 oz. can bamboo shoots
pinch salt
2 tablespoons (2½T) sherry
1 teaspoon Vesop
1 tablespoon (1¼T) cornflour (cornstarch)
4 oz. minced (ground) ham

Fried spinach

Wash the spinach thoroughly and drain off excess water, or defrost the frozen spinach. Heat the oil in a large saucepan, add the leaf spinach and fry over a fierce heat for 1 minute, stirring all the time, until the spinach softens. Add the salt and soya sauce, mix well and cook gently for another minute.

Serve immediately.

2 lb. fresh spinach or ¾ lb. frozen leaf spinach
1 tablespoon (1¼T) oil
1 teaspoon salt
1 tablespoon (1¼T) soya sauce

Cabbage with crab sauce

Wash and shred the cabbage. Cook in salted, boiling water for 2 minutes. Drain, reserving 2 tablespoons (2½T) of the water if no stock is available. Heat the oil and fry the cabbage and crushed garlic for 2 minutes. Add the soya sauce and sherry, mix well and cook for 1 minute.

Mix the cornflour (cornstarch) to a smooth paste with the stock or cabbage water, stir into the pan with the crab meat. Mix well and cook for 1 minute more.

Serve immediately.

1 lb. white cabbage
1 tablespoon (1¼T) oil
1 clove garlic
1 tablespoon (1¼T) soya sauce
1 tablespoon (1¼T) sherry
1 teaspoon cornflour (cornstarch)
2 tablespoons (2½T) stock or cabbage water
4 oz. can crab meat

Celery and mushrooms

Wash the celery and cut into 1 inch lengths. Wash the mushrooms and cut into thick slices. Heat the oil and fry the mushrooms for 1 minute, add the celery, salt, sugar, soya sauce and Vesop, mix well and cook for 5 minutes.

Serve immediately.

1 small head celery
½ lb. fresh mushrooms
2 tablespoons (2½T) oil or melted lard
1 teaspoon salt
1 teaspoon brown sugar
2 tablespoons (2½T) soya sauce
1 teaspoon Vesop

Fried celery cabbage

Wash the cabbage and shred finely. Heat the oil or lard and fry the cabbage for 3 minutes, stirring all the time. Add the salt, mixing well.

Wash the celery and cut into thin slices, add to the cabbage with 2 tablespoons (2½T) water; cook over a fierce heat, stirring all the time, for 2 minutes.

Serve immediately.

1 lb. Chinese cabbage or hard white
  cabbage
2 tablespoons (2½T) oil or melted lard
1 teaspoon salt
2 sticks celery

Braised bean sprouts

Wash the bean sprouts and dry well. Heat the oil and fry the sprouts over a fierce heat for 3 minutes, stirring all the time. Add the remaining ingredients, mix well.

Serve immediately.

1 lb. bean sprouts
1 tablespoon (1¼T) oil
1 teaspoon vinegar
pinch salt
1 tablespoon (1¼T) soya sauce if liked

Fried beans

Wash and string the beans, breaking them into 1 inch pieces. Heat the oil and fry the beans over a medium heat for 3 minutes.

Add the stock or water and salt, bring to the boil, remove from the heat and leave for 1 minute. Bring back to the boil and stir over a gentle heat for 2 minutes, or until all the water has been absorbed.

Add the soya sauce, mix well and serve immediately.

1 lb. string (green or snap) beans
1 tablespoon (1¼T) oil or melted lard
¼ pint (⅝ cup) water or stock
1 teaspoon salt
1 tablespoon (1¼T) soya sauce if liked

Sweet and sour carrots

Scrub the carrots and cut into 1 inch pieces; chop the onions. Heat the oil and fry the carrots and onions for 1 minute. Add ¼ pint (⅝ cup) water and bring to the boil, simmer for 5 minutes.

Mix the salt, cornflour (cornstarch), vinegar and sugar together, add the stock or water and add to the pan, bring to the boil, stirring all the time until thickened and translucent. Cook for 1 minute.

Serve immediately.

1 lb. young carrots
1 spring onion (scallion)
1 tablespoon (1¼T) oil
1 teaspoon salt
1 tablespoon (1¼T) cornflour (cornstarch)
2 tablespoons (2½T) vinegar
1 tablespoon (1¼T) brown sugar
½ pint (1¼ cups) stock or water

Fried bean curd

Break the bean curd into 1 inch pieces. Heat the oil and deep fry the bean curd for 2–3 minutes or until browned and crisp on the outside and soft in the centre.

Mix the cornflour (cornstarch) to a smooth paste with the remaining ingredients, put into a small pan and bring to the boil, stirring all the time until slightly thickened and translucent.

Add the bean curd and serve immediately.

½ lb. bean curd
deep fat for frying
1 tablespoon (1¼T) cornflour (cornstarch)
2 tablespoons (2½T) soya sauce
2 tablespoons (2½T) vinegar
1 tablespoon (1¼T) brown sugar
½ teaspoon Ve-tsin (monosodium glutamate)
¼ pint (⅝ cup) water

Bean curd with oyster sauce

Wash and slice the mushrooms. Heat the oil and fry the mushrooms over a fierce heat for 2 minutes, stirring all the time. Remove them from the pan.

Break the bean curd into small pieces and add to the remaining oil, cook gently for 2–3 minutes until browned on the outside. Add the oyster sauce and pepper, mix well and leave for 2 minutes. Add the mushrooms, mix well and gently heat through.

Serve immediately.

4 oz. fresh mushrooms
2 tablespoons (2½T) oil
1 lb. bean curd
3 tablespoons (3¾T) oyster sauce
pinch black pepper

Bean curd with haddock

Wipe the fish, heat the oil and fry the fish, whole, for 2 minutes. Sprinkle with the sherry, ginger and soya sauce. Cover the pan and heat gently for 5 minutes.

Chop the onions and break the bean curd into 1 inch pieces. Add to the fish with the salt and water. Bring to the boil, simmer for 5 minutes, then serve immediately.

½ lb. piece haddock fillet
1 tablespoon (1¼T) oil
1 tablespoon (1¼T) sherry
pinch ground ginger
2 teaspoons soya sauce
2 spring onions (scallions)
½ lb. bean curd
pinch salt
¼ pint (⅝ cup) water

Stuffed peppers

Wash and core the peppers; keeping them whole, remove the seeds. Put them into a large pan, cover with cold water, bring to the boil, drain.

Mix the pork, crushed garlic, soya sauce, cornflour (cornstarch) and sherry together, until evenly blended. Fill the peppers with the pork mixture. Place the peppers in a greased dish, cover and steam for 30 minutes.

Serve immediately.

4 green peppers
1 lb. lean pork, cooked and minced
1 clove garlic
1 tablespoon (1¼T) soya sauce
1 tablespoon (1¼T) cornflour (cornstarch)
1 tablespoon (1¼T) sherry

Chinese pickled cucumber

Peel the cucumber and cut into thin slices. Put the vinegar, sugar and ginger into a small pan, bring to the boil, pour over the cucumber and leave until quite cold.

Stir in sesame oil, if liked, at the last minute.

1 cucumber
2 tablespoons (2½T) vinegar
1 tablespoon (1¼T) brown sugar
1 teaspoon ground ginger
1 teaspoon sesame oil (optional)

Fried mixed vegetables

Thickly peel the turnip, peel the carrots and cut both into matchsticks; scrub the celery, wash the leeks and cut both into thin slices.

Heat the oil or lard and fry all the vegetables together for 3–4 minutes, over a medium heat, stirring all the time. Sprinkle with salt and vinegar, mix well and serve hot or cold sprinkled with sesame oil.

1 small turnip
2 large carrots
1 small head celery
2 medium leeks
1 tablesppon (1¼T) oil or melted lard
1 teaspoon salt
1 teaspoon wine vinegar
1 teaspoon sesame oil

Preparing the carrots and turnips for Fried mixed vegetables

Eggs

In China, hen's eggs are as vital to cooking as in the West. They are generally used as a combination ingredient rather than cooked and served on their own. Some soups will have a whole egg dropped into them, but it is not usually cooked, only slightly coagulated by the heat of the soup.

Some dishes contain whole, hard-boiled eggs which are split to allow the flavour of the juices from the main dish to penetrate the yolk (see Pork and Eggs, page 14).

The famous 100-year-old eggs of China are not, as their name might suggest, actually 100 years old, but are eggs preserved in lime. They are considered best when about $3\frac{1}{2}$ months old – or 100 *days*.

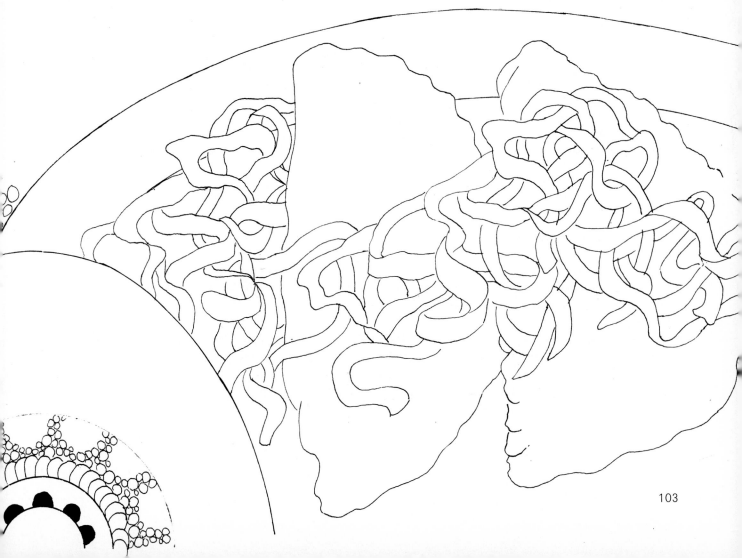

Scrambled eggs with prawns (shrimp)

Chop the prawns (shrimp) roughly; wash and chop the onion (scallion); wash and slice the mushrooms. Melt the fat and fry the prawns (shrimp), onions and mushrooms for 1 minute.

Beat the eggs, sherry, salt and pepper together until smooth. Pour on to the ingredients in the pan and stir briskly for 1–2 minutes until scrambled and set.

6 oz. peeled prawns (shrimp)
1 spring onion (scallion)
1 oz. fresh mushrooms
1 oz. (2T) lard or dripping (shortening)
6 eggs
3 tablespoons ($3\frac{3}{4}$T) sherry
1 teaspoon salt
pinch black pepper

Steamed eggs with pork

Mince (grind) the pork finely; wash and chop the onion (scallion) finely, add to the pork, eggs and salt. Beat well and gradually beat in the stock or milk. Pour into a greased bowl or soufflé dish. Steam for 20 minutes.

Remove from the steamer and sprinkle the top with soya sauce. Mince (grind) the ham and sprinkle over the top of the eggs.

Serve immediately from the bowl.

4 oz. pork
1 spring onion (scallion)
4 eggs
1 teaspoon salt
$\frac{1}{4}$ pint ($\frac{5}{8}$ cup) pork stock or milk
1 teaspoon soya sauce
1 oz. ham

Eggs with crab and bean sprouts

Chop the crab meat. Heat the fat and fry the crab, stirring all the time, for 1 minute. Wash and drain the bean sprouts, add to the crab and cook for 2–3 minutes.

Beat the eggs, salt and pepper together until smooth. Pour into the pan and stir gently over a low heat until the eggs are set.

Wash and finely chop the onions (scallions), sprinkle over the egg mixture and serve immediately.

7 oz. crab meat
1 oz. lard (shortening)
$\frac{1}{2}$ lb. bean sprouts
6 eggs
1 teaspoon salt
pinch black pepper
2 spring onions (scallions)

Egg wrapped dumplings

Wash and chop the onions (scallions); mince (grind) with the pork, and finely chop the ginger. Mix these with the soya sauce, beating well until evenly blended.

Beat the eggs and salt together until smooth. Heat some fat in a shallow frying pan. Drop 1 tablespoon ($1\frac{1}{4}$T) of the egg mixture in the centre of the pan and immediately place 1 teaspoon of the pork mixture in the centre. Fold the now set egg over and press the edges together. Lift out into another pan. Cover with stock and heat gently for 5 minutes.

Serve immediately.

2 spring onions (scallions)
$\frac{1}{2}$ lb. pork
$\frac{1}{2}$ oz. stem ginger
2 tablespoons ($2\frac{1}{2}$T) soya sauce
3 eggs
1 teaspoon salt
$\frac{1}{4}$ pint ($\frac{5}{8}$ cup) pork stock

Egg wrapped dumplings

Braised eggs

Cook the eggs in boiling water for 5 minutes, remove from the pan and leave under cold running water for 5 minutes. Remove the shells.

Mix the soya sauce and oil together. Heat gently. Add the eggs and turn in the mixture for 5 minutes or until brown.

Leave to cool in the mixture, remove and cut in quarters to serve.

6 eggs
4 tablespoons (5T) soya sauce
2 tablespoons (2½T) peanut or sunflower oil

Egg threads

Beat the eggs until smooth. Heat the oil in a large frying pan, but not too hot. Pour the eggs in gently, so that they form a thin layer over the base of the pan. Allow to set.

Remove from the pan, cool and cut into very thin strips, about 4 inches long. Use the rest of the egg in the same way.

Note: use egg threads as a garnish over such dishes as fried noodles, etc.

2 eggs
2 tablespoons (2½T) peanut or sunflower oil

Eggs for Chinese dishes

Egg and Ham dumplings

Mince (grind) the ham, mix with the eggs and breadcrumbs, beating well until smooth. Shape the mixture into small balls the size of golf balls.

Heat the fat until smoking and fry the dumplings four at a time until golden brown. Drain on kitchen paper and serve immediately.

1 lb. ham
4 eggs
2 oz. white breadcrumbs
1 teaspoon plain (all-purpose) flour
deep fat for frying

Steamed eggs with plaice (flounder)

Skin and bone the fish, mince (grind) twice. Add the eggs, salt, pepper, oil, lemon rind and stock or milk. Beat well until smooth. Put into a greased bowl or soufflé dish. Steam for 20 minutes.

Wash and finely chop the onions (scallions), and sprinkle over the top of the fish with the soya sauce.

Serve immediately.

1 lb. plaice (flounder) fillet
4 eggs
1 teaspoon salt
pinch black pepper
1 tablespoon ($1\frac{1}{4}$T) oil
grated rind of 1 lemon
$\frac{1}{4}$ pint ($\frac{5}{8}$ cup) fish or chicken stock, or milk
2 spring onions (scallions)
1 tablespoon ($1\frac{1}{4}$T) soya sauce

Eggs Fu Yung

Shred the meat finely and season with salt and pepper. Wash and chop the onions (scallions) finely; scrub and thinly slice the celery; wash the pea sprouts.

Melt a little fat in a large pan, add the meat shreds and stir well over a fierce heat for 1 minute. Add the onions (scallions), celery and pea sprouts, and mix well with the meat for 2 minutes. Add the soya sauce and sugar, mix well.

Remove the mixture from the pan and keep it hot. Beat the eggs and salt together until smooth. Pour into the greased pan and leave over a slow heat until the underside is set. Pile the meat and vegetable mixture in the centre and fold the egg over to make a half round. Cook gently for 2–3 minutes.

Serve immediately.

Note: to serve with sauce, mix 1 tablespoon (1¼T) cornflour (cornstarch) to a smooth paste with 2 tablespoons (2½T) cold water, add ½ pint (1¼ cups) stock and bring to the boil, stirring until thickened. Cook for 2–3 minutes. Pour over the eggs just before serving.

½ lb. meat – pork, chicken or ham
2 spring onions (scallions)
2 sticks celery
4 oz. pea sprouts
2 tablespoons (2½T) soya sauce
2 teaspoons brown sugar
8 eggs
1 teaspoon salt

Pork omelet

Cut the pork into paper thin slices and mix with the soya sauce. Heat the fat in a large frying pan, add the meat and fry over a fierce heat for 1 minute, stirring all the time.

Beat the eggs and salt together until smooth. Pour on to the meat and stir well until set.

Serve immediately.

Note: often a double quantity is made: one half is heated in stock and served as soup.

1 lb. lean pork
2 tablespoons (2½T) soya sauce or Vesop
1 oz. (2T) lard (shortening)
6 eggs
1 teaspoon salt

Pork omelet (left)
Eggs fu yung (right)

Rice and noodles

Rice falls into two clearly defined categories: dry rice – rice which has been boiled or steamed until all the liquid has been absorbed; and soft rice or congee, which is a small amount of rice cooked for about 40 minutes in a large amount of water, the result being rather like watery porridge. Like porridge, congee is eaten as the first meal of the day, usually in conjunction with salted fish or some other strongly flavoured food.

Dry rice can be either steamed or boiled, the latter being most popular in the West since the circular wooden steamers used for the purpose in China are not readily available everywhere.

Despite the fact that rice is the staple food of China it is not, as is assumed by Westerners, eaten with every dish regardless. The average meal of, perhaps, eight dishes will include one rice dish, which may be plain dry rice or a composite rice concoction.

The rice you normally use for cooking would be perfectly adequate in the following recipes.

Chinese noodles are made from a wheat starch dough and can vary in thickness from something akin to macaroni right down to the finest vermicelli. Pea starch noodles, used mainly for soups, are transparent, capable of absorbing a great deal of liquid and slip down so easily as to be almost unnoticeable.

But whatever their size, noodles are used in three ways: fried; in soup and in gravy or sauce.

Generally they are served as a mid-meal snack or suppertime dish, but in the northern regions they act as a staple food and are served with a sauce and often minced (ground) meat – this provides a very economical yet appetizing dish.

Steamed rice

Wash and drain the rice. Cook in boiling water for 3 minutes. Drain. Put the rice in a steaming tier and cook for 30 minutes. (If no steaming tier is available, use a nylon or hair sieve set in a wooden band.)

The Cantonese steam their rice in bowls; the rice is boiled for 5 minutes, drained and individual bowls are ¾ filled with half-cooked rice. It is then steamed for 1–1½ hours.

4 oz. (⅔ cup) long grain rice
1½–2 pints (3¾–5 cups) water

Boiled rice

Wash and drain the rice. Cook in the boiling water for 5 minutes, stirring occasionally to prevent sticking.

Reduce the heat to simmering, cover the pan and cook for 20 minutes or until all the water has been absorbed and the grains are quite separate.

½ lb. (1⅓ cups) long grain rice
¾ pint (1⅞ cups) water

White congee

Wash and drain the rice. Put into 1½–2 pints (3¾–5 cups) of boiling water, and bring back to the boil; simmer until the rice and water combine to make a thick 'porridgy' consistency.

It must be eaten piping hot.

4 oz. (⅔ cup) oval grain rice
1½–2 pints (3¾–5 cups) water

Fried rice

Season the rice well with salt and black pepper. Heat the oil or lard and fry the rice gently over a medium heat for about 10 minutes or until all the fat has been absorbed.

Beat the eggs until smooth and pour on to the rice in a thin stream, stirring all the time. Heat gently, stirring, until the egg is evenly distributed and set.

Serve immediately.

This is the simplest form of fried rice which, although very popular in the West, is not served in restaurants in China, and rarely in the Chinese home, except perhaps to the family's closest friends.

¾ lb. cooked, cold rice
2 tablespoons (2½ T) oil or melted lard
2 eggs

Fried rice with chicken

Heat the oil; peel and finely chop the onions; fry the onions (scallions) and garlic in the oil for 2 minutes over a medium heat. Add the rice, mix well and heat through.

Chop the chicken and mix with the soya sauce, add to the rice mixture and mix well. Beat the eggs until smooth, season with salt and pepper. Pour into the rice mixture in a thin stream, stirring all the time, until the eggs are cooked.

Serve immediately.

2 tablespoons (2½T) oil
2 spring onions (scallions)
1 clove crushed garlic
¾ lb. cooked rice
½ lb. cooked chicken
2 tablespoons (2½T) soya sauce
2 eggs
salt and pepper

Fried rice with pork and shrimp

Follow the preceding recipe, substituting 6 oz. finely chopped, cooked pork and 4 oz. cooked shrimps for the chicken.

Fried rice with crab and bamboo shoots

Follow the recipe for Fried Rice with Chicken, substituting 7 oz. canned drained crab meat and 4 oz. canned drained bamboo shoots, finely sliced, for the chicken.

Fried rice with mushrooms and pepper

Follow the recipe for Fried Rice with Chicken, substituting for the chicken 2 oz. chopped ham or pork, 6 oz. fresh and chopped or dried, soaked and sliced mushrooms and 1 green pepper, cored and sliced.

Fried rice with ham and bean sprouts

Follow the recipe for Fried Rice with Chicken, substituting 6 oz. chopped ham for the chicken and stirring in ½ lb. drained bean sprouts just before serving.

Fried rice with prawns (shrimps) and water chestnuts

Follow the recipe for Fried Rice with Chicken, substituting for the chicken 4 oz. peeled chopped prawns (shrimp) and 4 chopped water chestnuts.

Rice served, in typical Chinese fashion, as part of a meal (left)

Fried rice with ham and bean sprouts (below)

Soups

Unlike Western soups, which are served at the beginning of a meal, Chinese soups can be taken at any time between any one of the numerous dishes being served. At an ordinary meal, a communal bowl of soup is placed on the table, from which everyone takes a spoonful as and when they wish. The Fukien region is noted for its soups, and it is not uncommon for three or more different soups to be served in a meal consisting of ten dishes.

Chinese soups are made from a basic stock (see recipe page 118) whether pork, beef, chicken or ham, as they are in the West, but the proportion of meat to water is much higher than in the West, producing a tastier and richer liquid. This kind of soup can be served simply with the addition of, for instance, egg threads (see page 118) or with a more composite variety of titbits.

The soups of China are generally very light, with ingredients more flavoursome than substantial. And since water or tea is seldom served at a Chinese meal, soup serves as a welcome drink, particularly after a rich dish such as dumplings or deep fried prawns.

Chinese stock

Put the meats into a saucepan with the water. Bring gently to the boil; remove the scum, cover the pan and simmer slowly until the liquid has reduced by half. Cool, remove the fat and strain the stock.

Keep in a cool place for later use.

½ lb. chopped chicken
½ lb. chopped pork
1 pint (2½ cups) water

Veal or chicken stock

Make as above, using either all chicken or all veal.

Bone stock

Make as above, using good quality pork or veal bones.

Egg flower soup

Heat the stock to boiling point.

Beat the eggs and oil together until smooth. Wash and chop the onions finely. Pour the egg mixture into the boiling soup in a thin stream. The heat of the stock will set the egg immediately and it will form thin ribbons. Add the remaining ingredients and stir over a moderate heat for 2–3 minutes.

Serve immediately.

2 pints (5 cups) bone stock (see page 118)
2 eggs
1 teaspoon oil
2 spring onions (scallions)
2 tablespoons (2½ T) soya sauce or Vesop
1 teaspoon vinegar
½ teaspoon Ve-tsin (monosodium glutamate)
1 teaspoon salt
pinch black pepper

Bean sprout soup

Bring the stock to the boil. Cut the pork into paper-thin slices and add to the stock, simmer for 5 minutes. Wash and drain the sprouts, add to the stock, and simmer for another 5 minutes. Wash and chop the onions (scallions), add to the stock and simmer for 2–3 minutes. Stir in the soya sauce or Vesop and Ve-tsin.

Serve immediately.

2 pints (5 cups) Chinese stock (page 118)
4 oz. lean pork
½ lb. bean sprouts
2 spring onions (scallions)
2 teaspoons soya sauce or Vesop
½ teaspoon Ve-tsin (monosodium glutamate)

Mixed vegetable soup

Peel the carrots and turnip, shred or grate the flesh finely; grate the bamboo; wash and shred the cabbage; mix the salt with these vegetables. Slice the tomatoes. Fry these vegetables in a little oil for 5 minutes, stirring well to blend evenly. Add the water, mix well, then stir in the noodles. Simmer for 30 minutes.

Slice the pickles; wash and chop the onions (scallions), add with the pickles and pea sprouts to the cooking vegetables and cook for 5 minutes. Add the remaining ingredients and simmer for 10 minutes.

Serve immediately.

2 carrots
1 small turnip
3 oz. bamboo shoots
4 oz. white cabbage
1 teaspoon salt
2 large tomatoes
2 pints (5 cups) water
3 oz. (¾ cup) starch noodles
3 oz. Chinese pickles (cha tsai)
2 spring onions (scallions)
3 oz. pea sprouts
2 teaspoons salt
2 tablespoons (2½ T) Vesop
½ teaspoon Ve-tsin (monosodium glutamate)
pinch pepper

Ingredients for a mixed vegetable soup

Pork and watercress soup

Bring the stock to the boil and add the salt. Mix the cornflour (cornstarch) and water to a smooth paste, add the pork and mix well. Separate and add to the soup; simmer for 5 minutes.

Wash the watercress; wash and chop the onions, add to the stock with the remaining ingredients. Simmer for another 5 minutes.

Serve immediately.

2 pints (5 cups) bone stock (page 118)
1 teaspoon salt
2 teaspoons cornflour (cornstarch)
1 tablespoon (1¼T) water
4 oz. chopped pork
1 bunch watercress
2 spring onions (scallions)
2 tablespoons (2½T) soya sauce or Vesop
½ teaspoon Ve-tsin (monosodium glutamate)
pinch black pepper

Pork and watercress soup

Chinese ravioli soup

Bring the stock to the boil. Wash and chop the onions (scallions), add to the stock and simmer for 5 minutes. Add the salt, soya sauce and Ve-tsin to the stock.

Fry the ravioli in deep fat for 1–2 minutes or until crisp on the outside. Drain on kitchen paper. Put the ravioli in a large soup tureen and pour the stock over. The ravioli will rise to the top of the soup, which must be served immediately in order for the crispness to be felt in contrast to the hot liquid.

2 pints (5 cups) chicken stock (page 118)
2 spring onions (scallions)
1 teaspoon salt
1 tablespoon (1¼T) soya sauce
½ teaspoon Ve-tsin (monosodium glutamate)
6 oz. Chinese ravioli
deep fat for frying

Crab and vinegar soup

Remove all the meat from the crab, discarding the sac and "dead men's fingers"; chop the claw meat. Fry the meat in a little oil with the salt and ginger; slice the tomatoes, add to the crab and fry gently for 5 minutes. Add the chicken stock and simmer for 15 minutes.

Beat the eggs and add to the soup in a thin stream, so that they form ribbons. Add the remaining ingredients, stir well and serve immediately.

1 large cooked crab
1 teaspoon salt
1 teaspoon chopped ginger
2 tomatoes
2 pints (5 cups) chicken stock (page 118)
2 eggs
2 tablespoons (2½T) sherry
2 tablespoons (2½T) vinegar
1 teaspoon salt
2 tablespoons (2½T) Vesop
½ teaspoon Ve-tsin (monosodium glutamate)

Chicken and fish soup

Cut the fish into ½ inch pieces, removing the skin and bones. Mix the cornflour (cornstarch) and water to a smooth paste and add the fish, mixing well.

Bring the stock to the boil, add the fish, stir well to separate and simmer for 15 minutes. Slice the ham very thinly; wash and chop the onions, add to the pan and simmer for 5 minutes.

Add the remaining ingredients, stir well and serve immediately.

1 lb. white fish (sole or halibut)
1 tablespoon (1¼T) cornflour (cornstarch)
2 tablespoons (2½T) water
2 pints (5 cups) chicken stock (page 118)
2 oz. ham
3 spring onions (scallions)
1 teaspoon salt
2 slices green ginger
2 teaspoons (2½T) Vesop
1 tablespoon (1¼T) sherry
2 teaspoons vinegar
½ teaspoon Ve-tsin (monosodium glutamate)

Meat slice and bean curd soup

Cut the pork into paper thin slices. Mix the cornflour (cornstarch) and water to a smooth paste, add the meat, mix well.

Bring the stock to the boil with the salt. Add the meat, stirring to separate. Simmer for 5 minutes. Cut the bean curd into ½ inch pieces, add to the stock and simmer for another 5 minutes.

Add the remaining ingredients, stir well and serve immediately.

½ lb. lean pork
1 teaspoon cornflour (cornstarch)
1 tablespoon (1¼T) water
2 pints (5 cups) Chinese stock (page 118)
1 teaspoon salt
1 lb. bean curd
1 tablespoon (1¼T) sherry
2 tablespoon (2½T) soya sauce
½ teaspoon Ve-tsin (monosodium glutamate)

Meat slice and cucumber soup

Cut the meat into paper thin slices. Mix the cornflour (cornstarch), 1 tablespoon (1¼T) soya sauce and the sherry to a smooth paste. Add the meat and mix well.

Bring the stock to the boil with the salt. Add the meat, stirring to separate, simmer for 5 minutes. Peel and thinly slice the cucumber. Add to the stock with remaining soya sauce and simmer for 2–3 minutes.

Serve immediately.

½ lb. lean pork
2 teaspoons cornflour (cornstarch)
2 tablespoons (2½T) soya sauce
1 teaspoon sherry
2 pints (5 cups) Chinese stock (page 118)
½ teaspoon salt
1 small cucumber

Chicken and fried noodle soup

Cut the chicken into paper thin slices; slice the mushrooms and bamboo shoots. Bring the stock to the boil, add the chicken, mushrooms and bamboo shoots, simmer for 10 minutes.

Cook noodles in a pan of boiling water for 2 minutes. Drain and arrange in a soup tureen. Wash and chop the onion (scallion), add to the stock, and simmer for 2–3 minutes.

Pour the soup over the noodles and serve immediately.

6 oz. chicken breast
1 oz. fresh mushrooms
1 oz. bamboo shoots
1 pint (2½ cups) chicken stock (page 118)
4 oz. fried noodles
1 spring onion (scallion)

Shrimp and cabbage soup

Mince (grind) or finely chop the shrimps and ginger, mix with the egg whites and beat well until smooth.

Wash and shred or grate the cabbage and celery. Bring the stock or water to the boil, add the cabbage and celery and cook for 5 minutes.

Mix the cornflour (cornstarch) and water to a smooth paste, add to the soup, stirring until slightly thickened. Add the shrimps, stir well and simmer for 2–3 minutes. Wash and chop the onions (scallions), add to the soup, simmer for 2–3 minutes.

Serve immediately.

6 oz. peeled shrimps
1 slice ginger
2 egg whites
½ lb. white cabbage
4 oz. celery
2 pints (5 cups) stock or water
2 tablespoons (2½T) cornflour (cornstarch)
3 tablespoons (3¾T) water
2 spring onions (scallions)

Asparagus soup

Cut the chicken into paper thin slices. Mix the cornflour (cornstarch) and water to a smooth paste and add to the chicken, mixing well. Bring the stock to the boil, then add the chicken mixture, stirring to separate. Simmer for 15 minutes.

Cut the asparagus in half and add to the stock with the asparagus liquid. Simmer for 10 minutes. Stir in the sherry and Ve-tsin.

Serve immediately.

½ lb. chicken breast
1 tablespoon (1¼T) cornflour (cornstarch)
1 tablespoon (1¼T) water
2 pints (5 cups) chicken stock
10 oz. can asparagus tips
1 tablespoon (1¼T) sherry
½ teaspoon Ve-tsin (monosodium glutamate)

Abalone and green pea soup

Abalone and green pea soup

Slice the mushrooms and soak in boiling water for 30 minutes.

Bring the stock to the boil. Shred the pork and add to the stock, simmering for 5 minutes. Add the peas and mushrooms and simmer for 5 minutes.

Drain the abalone, keeping the juice, and cut the abalone into small pieces; add to the stock with the juice, soya sauce or Vesop, stir and serve immediately.

4 dried mushrooms

2 pints (5 cups) pork stock

4 oz. lean pork

½ lb. fresh green peas or 4 oz. frozen, defrosted

1 small can abalone

1 tablespoon (1¼T) soya sauce or Vesop

123

Sour soup

Bring the stock gently to the boil. Mix the soya sauce, cornflour (cornstarch), vinegar, salt, Ve-tsin and pepper to a smooth paste. Add to the soup, stirring all the time until slightly thickened. Simmer for 5 minutes.

Beat the eggs until smooth and pour in a thin stream into the stock, so that they form ribbons. Add chopped meat or vegetables, if liked.

Serve immediately.

2 pints (5 cups) chicken stock (page 118)
2 tablespoons (2½T) soya sauce or Vesop
2 tablespoons (2½T) cornflour (cornstarch)
3 tablespoons (3¾T) vinegar
1 teaspoon salt
½ teaspoon Ve-tsin (monosodium glutamate)
pinch pepper
3 eggs
6 ozs. chopped, cooked meat or vegetables (optional)

Sweetcorn and pork soup

Bring the stock gently to the boil. Mince (grind) the pork and add to the stock with the ginger. Simmer for 30 minutes. Drain the corn and add to the stock. Simmer for 10 minutes.

Beat the egg until smooth, pour into the stock in a thin stream, stir, then add the sherry or brandy and Ve-tsin.

Serve immediately.

2 pints (5 cups) Chinese stock (page 118)
½ lb. lean pork
1 small piece ginger
10 oz. can sweet corn
1 egg
1 teaspoon sherry or brandy
½ teaspoon Ve-tsin (monosodium glutamate)

Clear duck soup

Wash and skin the duck. Put into a large saucepan with the water, bring to the boil, remove the scum, cover with a tight fitting lid and simmer for 2–2½ hours.

Remove the ham rind and add the piece of gammon to the pan.

Slice the bamboo shoots and mushrooms; wash the onions (scallions). Add to the pan with the salt, bring back to the boil and simmer for 30 minutes.

Serve the soup in a large tureen with the ham sliced, and the mushrooms and bamboo shoots arranged on top of the duck.

The correct way to eat this dish is to pinch off pieces of the meat from the carcass with chopsticks. These taste even better when dipped in a small bowl of soya sauce before eating.

5 lb. duck
4 pints (10 cups) water
½ lb. piece gammon
4 oz. bamboo shoots
8 Chinese (dried) mushrooms
2 spring onions (scallions)
1 tablespoon (1¼T) salt

Bird's nest soup

Soak the bird's nest in boiling water for 4 hours. Drain and remove feathers. Put into a large pan with the sherry and water, bring to the boil, then simmer for 30 minutes.

Add the stock and salt to the bird's nest mixture, bring to the boil and simmer for 15 minutes.

Mince (grind) the chicken twice, add the egg whites and beat well until smooth. Pour the chicken mixture into the stock in a thin stream, stir well and simmer for 10 minutes. Pour into a large bowl, sprinkle with chopped ham, and serve immediately.

4 oz. dried bird's nest
1 tablespoon (1¼T) sherry
½ pint (1¼ cups) water
2 pints (5 cups) chicken stock (page 118)
3 oz. chicken breast
3 egg whites
1 teaspoon salt
1 oz. chopped ham

Watermelon soup

Cut the mushrooms into small pieces and soak in boiling water for 1 hour. Cut the bamboo into thin slices; shred or mince (grind) the ham.

Bring the stock to the boil. Mince the chicken and pork, add to the stock and simmer for 10 minutes. Add the drained mushrooms, bamboo shoots and ham, mix well and add the Ve-tsin and peas.

Cut the top from the melon and scoop out the seeds and some of the pulp. Pour the soup into the melon and replace the top. Stand the melon in a basin and steam for about 1½ hours or until the melon is cooked.

The correct way to serve this soup is to place the melon on the table and scoop out soup and flesh, cutting the peel down as the level of soup is lowered.

1 oz. dried mushrooms
4 oz. bamboo shoots
4 oz. green peas
4 oz. lean ham
1 pint (2½ cups) chicken stock
6 oz. chicken
6 oz. pork
½ teaspoon Ve-tsin (monosodium glutamate)
4 lb. watermelon

Fish ball soup

Skin the fish and remove any bones; mince (grind) the flesh finely. Mince (grind) the pork twice and mix with the fish, cornflour (cornstarch) and water. Beat until smooth. Shape the mixture into balls. Bring the stock to the boil, add the fish balls and simmer for 15 minutes.

Wash and chop the onion (scallion), add to the soup and simmer for another 5 minutes. Add the remaining ingredients, stir well and serve immediately.

½ lb. white fish (whiting, sole, halibut, etc.)
2 oz. lean pork
1 tablespoon (1¼ T) cornflour (cornstarch)
1 tablespoon (1¼ T) water
2 pints (5 cups) chicken stock (page 118)
2 spring onions (scallions)
1 teaspoon salt
2 tablespoons (2½ T) Vesop
2 tablespoons (2½ T) sherry
1 tablespoon (1¼ T) vinegar
½ teaspoon Ve-tsin (monosodium glutamate)
pinch pepper

Chicken, ham and mushroom soup

Cut the mushrooms into small pieces and soak in ½ pint (1¼ cups) water for one hour. Bring the stock to the boil.

Shred the ham and add to the stock. Simmer for 10 minutes. Add the mushrooms and their liquor. Slice the chicken thinly and add to the stock. Simmer for 10 minutes.

Add the remaining ingredients, stir well and serve immediately.

8 Chinese mushrooms
4 oz. ham
2 pints (5 cups) chicken stock (page 118)
4 oz. chicken
1 teaspoon salt
1 tablespoon (1¼ T) Vesop
1 tablespoon (1¼ T) sherry
½ teaspoon Ve-tsin (monosodium glutamate)
pinch pepper

Chicken noodle soup

Cut the chicken and bamboo shoots into 2 inch long matchsticks. Bring the stock to the boil, add the chicken and bamboo and simmer for 10 minutes.

Add the noodle and salt; simmer for another 5 minutes. Add the Vesop, sherry and pepper. Chop the ham finely, add to the soup. Simmer for 3 minutes.

Serve immediately.

4 oz. chicken breast
2 oz. bamboo shoots
2 pints (5 cups) chicken stock (page 118)
3 oz. egg noodle
1 teaspoon salt
1 tablespoon (1¼ T) Vesop
1 tablespoon (1¼ T) sherry
pinch of pepper
2 oz. ham

Watermelon soup

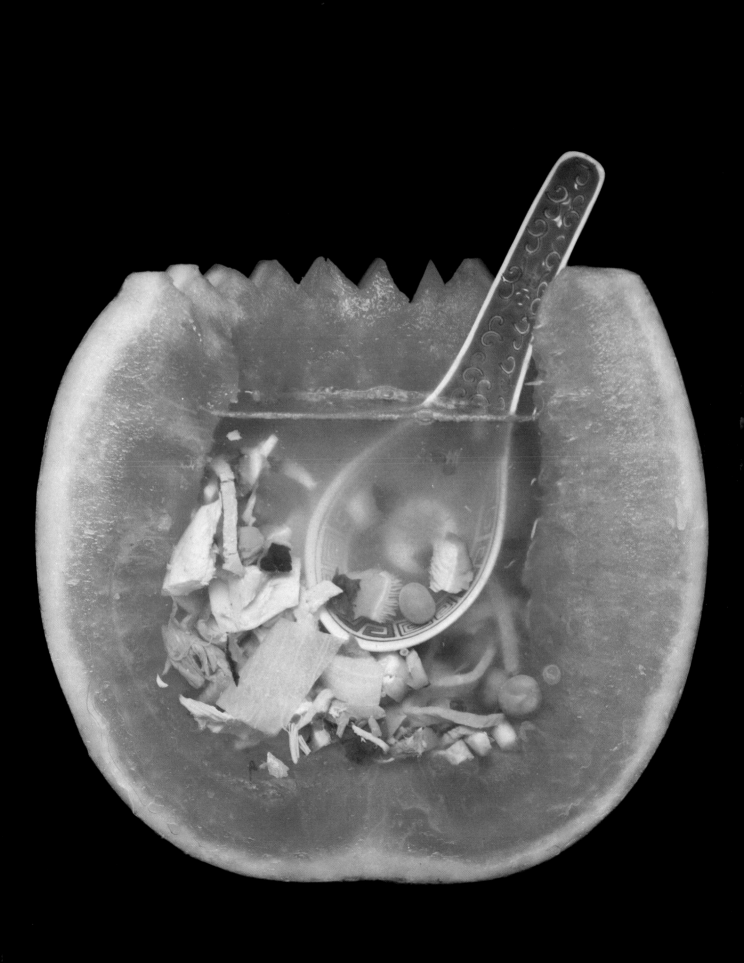

精品

Special dishes

Brazier lamb

Cut the meat into very fine slices and divide evenly between each guest's plate. Break one egg into each bowl. Crush the garlic and put into a large screw top jar. Chop the onions (scallions) very finely and add with the remaining ingredients to the garlic. Secure the lid and shake vigorously to blend the ingredients evenly. Divide this into further small bowls, one per person.

At this stage the guests take over. A charcoal fire, which has been burning until glowing stage is reached, is placed on the table and covered with a fine mesh rack to prevent the pieces of meat from falling into the embers.

Next, each guest is served one or two plates of meat, one bowl containing the egg and another bowl containing sauce. The idea is to use very long chopsticks (fondue forks make an ideal tool for the uninitiated), and to pick up a piece of meat, hold it over the fire for a few seconds (no more, as the intense heat soon cooks the fine slices), and dip it first into the raw egg, then into the sauce, before eating.

Like outdoor barbecues, this is an informal yet exciting method of eating and one which is guaranteed to break the ice in situations where most of the guests do not know each other. The meal does tend to go on, though, as the fascination of doing one's own cooking at someone else's table seems to increase the appetite, and it is sometimes difficult to keep track of how much one has actually consumed. Hence an inevitable feeling of over-indulgence accompanies the end of the meal!

1 large leg of lamb or 1 tenderloin per person
1 egg per person
4 cloves garlic
5 spring onions (scallions)
4 tablespoons (5T) soya sauce
4 tablespoons (5T) fermented soya paste
4 tablespoons (5T) sweet soya bean jam or redcurrant jelly, dissolved
2 teaspoons (2¼ teaspoons) chilli sauce
4 tablespoons (5T) oil

Velveteen of pork

Cut the meat into ½ inch cubes, put into a pan with the chicken stock, bring to the boil, cover and simmer very gently for about 2 hours, or until the pork is falling apart. Drain off any remaining stock.

Heat the oil in a deep saucepan, add the pork and fry over a fierce fire, stirring all the time for 4–5 minutes. Add the soya sauce, sherry, sugar, salt and soya paste. Mix well and continue to fry the mixture over a very low heat for about 10 minutes, stirring all the time until the ingredients blend together to form a thick, paste-like substance.

Serve cold on snippets of toasted or fried bread as starters.

Note: the velveteen can be stored in a screw top jar and a tea-spoonful added to vegetable dishes for flavour, rather like our own potted meats which, although cooked slightly differently, produce a softened, cooked meat paste.

2 lb. pork tenderloin
½ pint (1¼ cups) chicken stock (page 118)
2 tablespoons (2½T) peanut oil
3 tablespoons (3¾T) soya sauce
2 tablespoons (2½T) sherry
pinch brown sugar
pinch salt
½ teaspoon fermented soya bean paste

Firepot

Bone the chicken and cut all the meat into very fine Chinese slices. Arrange on several plates. Skin the fish and cut the flesh into paper-thin slices. Wash the liver, remove the membranes and cut the flesh into paper-thin slices. Soak the noodles in hot water for at least 30 minutes before serving. Trim the onions (scallions) and cut into short lengths. Heat the stock to boiling just before serving. Arrange all the ingredients separately on several plates.

Put the soya sauce, crushed garlic, chopped ginger, chilli sauce, paste and oil into a large screw top jar and shake vigorously until all the ingredients are evenly blended. Divide evenly between the guests' individual bowls.

The next step is purely guest participation. The Chinese use a special pot called a boiling fire pot which is a large brass bowl, the centre of which is shaped into a tall funnel. The funnel is filled with charcoal, and the surrounding pot then filled with boiling stock and placed in the centre of the table with all the raw, prepared ingredients surrounding it. It is very difficult to get these pots in the West, but I have found that a large shallow casserole dish placed on a table spirit burner makes an ideal substitute, with another spirit burner keeping the extra stock hot until it is needed to replenish the cooking pot.

To eat this great assortment of goodies, one takes a pair of chopsticks or a spoon and fork and selects an item of food, dips it momentarily in the boiling stock, then transfers it to one's own sauce bowl before eating. As for Brazier Lamb, one needs time, but like any communal cooking, the fire pot quickly dispenses with formality.

1 chicken
2 lb. pork or lamb tenderloin
2 lb. sole or plaice (flounder)
¾ lb. lamb's liver
½ lb. pea starch noodles
1 bunch spring onions (scallions)
2 pints (5 cups) chicken stock (page 118)
6 tablespoons (7½T) soya sauce
3 cloves garlic
1 tablespoon (1¼T) fresh chopped ginger
2 teaspoons (2½ teaspoons) chilli sauce
6 tablespoons (7½T) fermented soya bean paste
6 tablespoons (7½T) oil

Shark's fin with crab

Cover the shark's fins with boiling water, and leave to stand overnight. Drain and put into a pan with enough chicken stock to cover, bring gently to the boil, reduce the heat and simmer for about 2 hours or until the fins are completely softened. Drain.

Pick the crabs or drain the liquid from the cans. Beat the eggs and mix with the crab meat. Season with salt. Heat the fat until smoking, add the crab and egg mixture and fry over a fierce heat, stirring all the time for 2–3 minutes. Add the shark's fins and fry for a further 2 minutes.

Serve immediately.

Note: this is, of course, another stir fried dish, but it is the ingredients which make it so much of a speciality and not the method of cooking, as is the case with Firepot and Brazier Lamb.

10 oz. skinless shark's fins
chicken stock (page 118)
2 crabs or 14 oz. canned crab meat
2 eggs
1 teaspoon salt
2 tablespoons (2½T) oil or melted lard (shortening)

Dim sum

Nearly all the other recipes in this book fall into clearly defined categories. Those in this chapter do not, but come under the general heading of *dim sum*, meaning literally, 'dot the heart'. A rough translation might be 'fill a gap' – dim sum are snacks, appetite-bridgers, which you can eat between meals. They are served at any time of the day and are the nearest Chinese equivalent to Western pastries.

In this section you will find a grand medley of recipes. Steamed dumplings, fried onion cakes, the famous spring rolls – so called because they are eaten in the spring, soon after the Old Chinese Year.

Some of the recipes given make use of hun t'un skin (pronounced one ton) and this is obtainable from most Chinese supermarkets, as indeed are all the ingredients not usually found in general supermarkets.

Boiled pastry balls

Mince (grind) the pork and mix in the soya sauce and sherry. Chop the onion (scallion) finely and add to the pork with the sesame oil, cornflour (cornstarch) and salt. Beat well until evenly blended.

Mix the flour and hot water together to make a soft dough, adding more water if necessary. Divide the dough into 24 pieces and shape each into a ball. Make a hole in the centre of each ball and press some of the pork filling into the middle. Shape the dough around the filling and pinch the edges together. Drop the balls into a large pan of salted boiling water, allow to come back to the boil and boil for 5 minutes. Add ½ pint cold water to the pan, bring back to the boil and boil for another 3 minutes.

Drain the balls and serve four or more to each person with a little of the boiling water. Use a spoon to eat the balls, in order to catch the juices from the centre as the first bite is taken.

½ lb. lean pork
2 tablespoons (2½T) soya sauce
1 teaspoon sherry
1 spring onion (scallion)
few drops sesame oil
1 tablespoon (1¼T) cornflour (cornstarch)
pinch salt
½ lb. (2 cups) rice flour
about ¼ pint (⅝ cup) hot water

Steamed rolls

Cream the yeast and add to the water, knead into the flour until smooth and elastic; this takes about 5 minutes. Put into a clean bowl and leave, covered, in a warm place for about 1½ hours or until the dough has doubled its original size.

Turn on to a floured surface and knead lightly. Divide into two pieces and roll out each to an oblong about 15 inches long by 4 inches wide. Sprinkle with salt and oil. Roll each piece up from the long side to make two sausage shapes. Cut each into short lengths and leave in a warm place for about 10 minutes.

Steam the rolls in a steaming tier for 20 minutes.

Note: these rolls can successfully be stored in a cold place and reheated without loss of flavour or texture.

½ oz. fresh yeast
1 pint (2½ cups) warm water
1½ lb. (6 cups) plain (all-purpose) flour
salt
oil

Pasties

Fry the beef in the oil for 10 minutes. Chop the onions (scallions) and cabbage finely, add to the pan and cook for 2–3 minutes. Add the soya sauce and salt, mix well and leave until cold.

Mix the flour and egg together with enough water to make a soft dough. Turn on to a floured surface and knead lightly. Roll out very thinly and cut into 3 inch rounds. Place a little of the mixture in the centre of each round, dampen the edges with water and press together to seal.

Fry the pasties in the oil for 3 minutes, turning them once during cooking. Add the hot stock or water, cover the pan and simmer for 5 minutes.

Drain and serve.

¾ lb. minced (ground) beef
2 tablespoons (2½T) oil
6 spring onions (scallions)
4 oz. white cabbage heart
1 tablespoon (1¼T) soya sauce
1 teaspoon salt
¾ lb. (3 cups) plain (all-purpose) flour
1 egg
½ pint (1¼ cups) water
2 tablespoons (2½T) oil
¼ pint (⅝ cup) hot stock or water

Spring rolls

Mix the pork and shrimps together. Fry in oil for 2 minutes. Wash and finely chop the onions (scallions); drain the bean sprouts and add both to the pork. Mix well and cook for 2 minutes. Stir in the soya sauce, salt and sugar.

Mix the flour, water and egg to a smooth batter. Using a heavy based frying pan, lightly greased, make 16 very thin pancakes, cooked on one side only. Place some of the mixture in the centre. Fold the edge nearest you to the centre, fold both sides in to the centre, then roll up, sealing last edge with a little water. Make all the rolls like this, then fry in hot, deep fat for about 5 minutes, turning the rolls during cooking to ensure even browning.

Drain and serve hot.

½ lb. minced (ground), lean pork
4 oz. peeled shrimps
1 tablespoon (1¼T) oil
2 spring onions (scallions)
½ lb. bean sprouts
1 tablespoon (1¼T) soya sauce
1 teaspoon salt
pinch brown sugar
½ lb. (2 cups) flour
1 pint (2½ cups) water
1 egg
deep fat for frying

Spring rolls

Egg rolls

Egg rolls

Beat the eggs, flour and water together to make a smooth batter. Using a heavy-based 10 inch frying pan, make thin pancakes, cooking each on one side only.

Place a spoonful of filling in the centre and roll into parcels as for spring rolls. Deep fry the rolls for about 5 minutes, turning each during cooking to brown evenly.

Drain and cut each in half before serving.

6 eggs
3 oz. ($\frac{3}{4}$ cup) flour
$\frac{1}{2}$ pint (1$\frac{1}{4}$ cups) water
filling as for spring rolls (page 135)
deep fat for frying

Fried onion cakes

Knead the flour and water together to make a soft dough. Divide into six and shape each piece into a round about 12 inches across.

Wash and finely chop the onions (scallions). Spread 1 tablespoon (1$\frac{1}{4}$T) melted fat over each round and sprinkle $\frac{1}{6}$ of the chopped onions (scallions) over each round. Sprinkle each with about $\frac{1}{2}$ teaspoon salt and roll up tightly like a pancake. Fold each in half and twist into an upstanding spiral. Flatten with a rolling pin and re-roll to a round about 6 inches across.

Fry each cake in shallow oil over a medium heat for 2 minutes on each side. Reduce the heat to very low, cover the pan and cook each cake for another 3 minutes on each side.

Cut each round into six wedges and serve piping hot.

1 lb. (4 cups) flour
1 pint (2$\frac{1}{2}$ cups) water
2 bunches spring onions (scallions)
6 tablespoons (7$\frac{1}{2}$T) melted lard
  (shortening)
salt

Fried hun t'un

Cut out 2 inch rounds from the paste. Mince (grind) the pork, add soya sauce, sugar and salt, mix well and leave for 10 minutes. Defrost the spinach and squeeze in a clean, dry cloth to get rid of excess moisture. Add the pork and mix well.

Place a little of the mixture in the centre of each round, dampen the edges and press together to seal. Drop the *hun t'un* into deep fat and fry for about 5 minutes, turning during cooking to brown evenly.

Drain and serve hot.

Note: *Hun T'un* paste or skin, as it is sometimes called, is usually available from most Chinese stores. The correct pronunciation is 'one ton pay'.

1 lb. hun t'un paste
1 lb. streaky pork
2 tablespoons (2½T) soya sauce
1 teaspoon brown sugar
1 teaspoon salt
12 oz. packet leaf spinach
deep fat for frying

Sweet and sour hun t'un

Cut out 3 inch rounds from the paste. Mix the beef, soya sauce, ginger, salt and brown sugar. Place a little in centre of each round and seal the edges as for fried *hun t'un*. Cook the *hun t'un* in salted boiling water for 10 minutes. Drain.

Meanwhile make the sauce: mix the cornflour (cornstarch) to a smooth paste with the stock or water, vinegar, brown sugar and soya sauce. Mix well and bring gently to the boil, stirring until slightly thickened. Pour over the *hun t'un*.

Serve immediately.

½ lb. hun t'un paste
½ lb. minced (ground) pork or beef
1 tablespoon (1¼T) soya sauce
pinch ground ginger
pinch salt
pinch brown sugar
1 tablespoon (1¼T) cornflour (cornstarch)
3 tablespoons (3¾T) stock or water
2 tablespoons (2½T) vinegar
2 tablespoons (2½T) brown sugar
2 tablespoons (2½T) soya sauce

Sweets

This is a particularly small section since the Chinese do not eat sweet things in the same way as Westerners. They do not have puddings, desserts, sweets, or whatever other name you choose to call them, at the end of a meal as we do; instead they have the odd sweet item to add variety, perhaps in a many course meal, or sometimes to nibble between meals.

Apart from fresh fruits, dried nuts and fruit, there are the sweet dishes proper (those eaten during a meal), and also sweet Tien hsin or pastries, of which there are so many as to be confusing. Here are just a few ideas.

Jujube cake

Put the jujubes into a pan, cover with cold water and bring to the boil; simmer for 1 hour or until soft. Drain, then remove the skins and stones. If using dates, remove the stones and heat the dates slightly to soften the fruit. Beat the fruit to form a paste. Add the rice flour and knead together to make a soft dough.

Roll out to $\frac{1}{4}$ inch thick and cut out small shapes using fancy cutters.

Steam the cakes in a steaming tier or on a greased, fine mesh rack over a pan of boiling water for 5 minutes.

Note: the cakes will remain soft if glutinous rice flour is used. If unobtainable, use ordinary rice flour, but do not be alarmed when the cakes harden after cooking.

½ lb. jujubes (hung tsou) or dates
½ lb. glutinous rice flour

Wheat cakes

Knead the flour and water together to make a soft dough. Roll out *very* thinly and cut out 24 rounds, each 2 inches in diameter. Brush 12 of the rounds with oil and press the other 12 rounds on top. Roll each to a larger round about 6 inches across.

Using a heavy based frying pan, lightly greased, fry each round over a low heat for 3 minutes on each side, under a tight fitting lid.

Pile the cooked wheat cakes, sometimes called doilies, on a plate and serve covered with a cloth. To eat the wheat cakes, separate each layer; this is easily done because of the oil used to sandwich them together.

¾ lb. (3 cups) flour
¾ pint (1⅞ cups) almost boiling water
3 tablespoons (3¾ T) oil

Almond tea jelly

Mix the almonds and rice in a bowl with 2 pints (5 cups) cold water, cover and leave for 2 hours. Strain through a fine muslin into a large bowl. Add the milk and mix well.

Stand the bowl in a large saucepan with enough boiling water to come halfway up the sides of the bowl. Cover and simmer for 2 hours, stirring occasionally.

Add the sugar, stir well and leave to cool slightly. Mix the gelatin with 2 tablespoons (2½T) hot water until dissolved. Stir into the milk mixture when almost cold. Mix well and pour into a shallow serving dish. Leave until set.

4 oz. (½ cup) ground almonds
2 tablespoons (2½T) ground rice
½ pint (1¼ cups) milk
2 tablespoons (2½T) sugar
1 teaspoon gelatin

Rice pudding

Simmer the rice in the water for 20 minutes or until all the liquid has been absorbed. Add the milk and sugar, mix well and cook for a further 10 minutes, stirring occasionally to prevent sticking.

Slice the large fruits and halve the small ones before arranging in the base of a shallow dish or tin (I have found a 7-inch round cake tin with a loose base ideal for this). Pour the rice gently on top of the fruit so as not to disturb the fruit. Press the rice down firmly and cover with greased paper. Stand the tin in a saucepan of boiling water and simmer for about 2½ hours.

Remove the paper and invert the tin on to a plate. Shake the contents on to the plate – the pudding should unmould in one piece.

Eat whilst still hot.

¾ lb. (2 cups) round grain rice
1 pint (2½ cups) water
¼ pint (⅝ cup) milk
4 oz. (½ cup) sugar
variety candied fruits

Fried sweet potato

Thickly peel the potato and cut into sticks about ½ inch wide and 2–3 inches long – similar to chips. Dry the sticks on a clean towel and fry them in the oil for about 4 minutes or until golden brown and crisp. Drain and pile on a large dish. Heat the syrup and pour over the chips.

Serve immediately.

Note: Sweet potatoes are usually very large, often as much as 1 foot long. For this dish the smaller ones, if obtainable, are easier to handle.

1 lb. sweet potato
shallow oil for frying
6 tablespoons (7½ T) syrup

Rice pudding with sweet potato

Index

Acknowledgments

The following colour illustrations by courtesy of:

Barnaby's Picture Library:	page 35
Brown & Polson:	page 58
Bryce Attwell:	pages 19, 62, 82 below, 83, 95, 115
Conway Picture Library:	page 114
Paul Kemp:	pages 2–3, 6–7, 22, 23, 30, 31, 86–7, 91, 127
John Lee:	pages 15, 55, 59, 63, 82 above, 90, 94, 119, 123
Neil Lorimer:	pages 11, 14, 26, 27, 50, 51, 54

The following black and white illustrations by courtesy of:

The Bodley Head:	pages 52–3, 65, 73, 76–7, 85
Brown and Polson:	page 125
Bryce Attwell:	page 41
David Davis:	pages 42, 43, 46, 66, 67, 71, 72, 79, 101, 120, 141
Flour Advisory Bureau:	page 136
Paul Kemp:	pages 48, 69, 97, 106, 108
Michael Leale:	pages 28, 29, 36, 37, 40, 61
John Lee:	page 105
Neil Lorimer:	pages 4, 16, 17, 18, 20, 21
Planter's Peanut Oil:	page 109